MW01618179

timotion

DEWI LEWIS
PUBLISHING

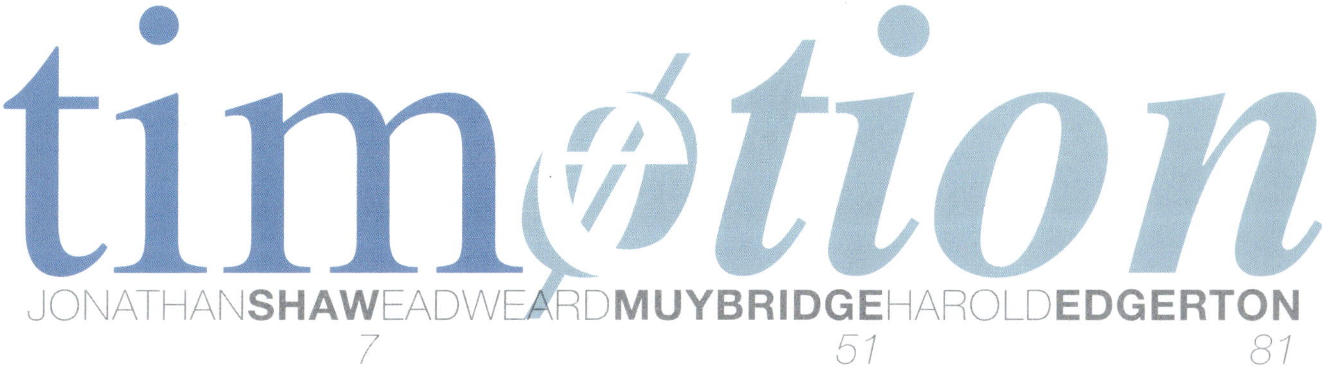
timemotion
JONATHANSHAWEADWEARDMUYBRIDGEHAROLDEDGERTON
7
51
81

Preface

This book, a collaboration between Dewi Lewis Publishing, Birmingham Library Services and Birmingham Museums & Art Gallery, celebrates the exhibition 'Time I Motion', held at Birmingham Museum & Art Gallery from July to September 2003, which brought together the work of three photographers, Eadweard Muybridge, Harold Edgerton and Jonathan Shaw. All three have links with Birmingham: Muybridge being a visitor and lecturer in the city in 1890; Edgerton having the first exhibition of his astonishing high-speed photographs made in the 1930s and 40s shown there in the 1970s; and Shaw being a Birmingham-based photographer whose subject matter includes the city and its people.

Central to the project was Jonathan Shaw's commission to produce two site-specific new pieces for the exhibition. Shaw observed and documented the movement of visitors within a range of gallery spaces at Birmingham Museum & Art Gallery to produce the new works, a computer interactive and a spectacular large print, over thirteen metres long, which ran the length of the gallery in which it was shot – the largest single photograph ever displayed in the Museum. Shaw's work was shown alongside plates from Muybridge's revolutionary 11 volume Animal Locomotion **(1887), part of Birmingham Central Library's important photography collections, and key examples of Edgerton's high-speed photographs generously lent by Geoffrey W. Holt. Together the work of these three photographers demonstrates the extraordinary potential of the photographic image to explore and capture movement and the passage of time.**

JONATHAN**SHAW**

Kinematographs.

(kəinī·mătəgrɑf, kəinĭmæ·təgrɑf).

[C19 (earlier spelling: *kinematograph*): from Gk *kinēma* motion + -GRAPH]

Jonathan Shaw photographs time. Of course every photographer makes images of time, by trying to arrest it. Capturing a moment that is, in fact, precisely out of time. Shaw has always been concerned to go beyond the

movement as something fluid. After all we do not perceive movement as a series of stills, nor exactly as cinema's 24 frames per second illusion of movement. Surely instead we sense movement as continuous in

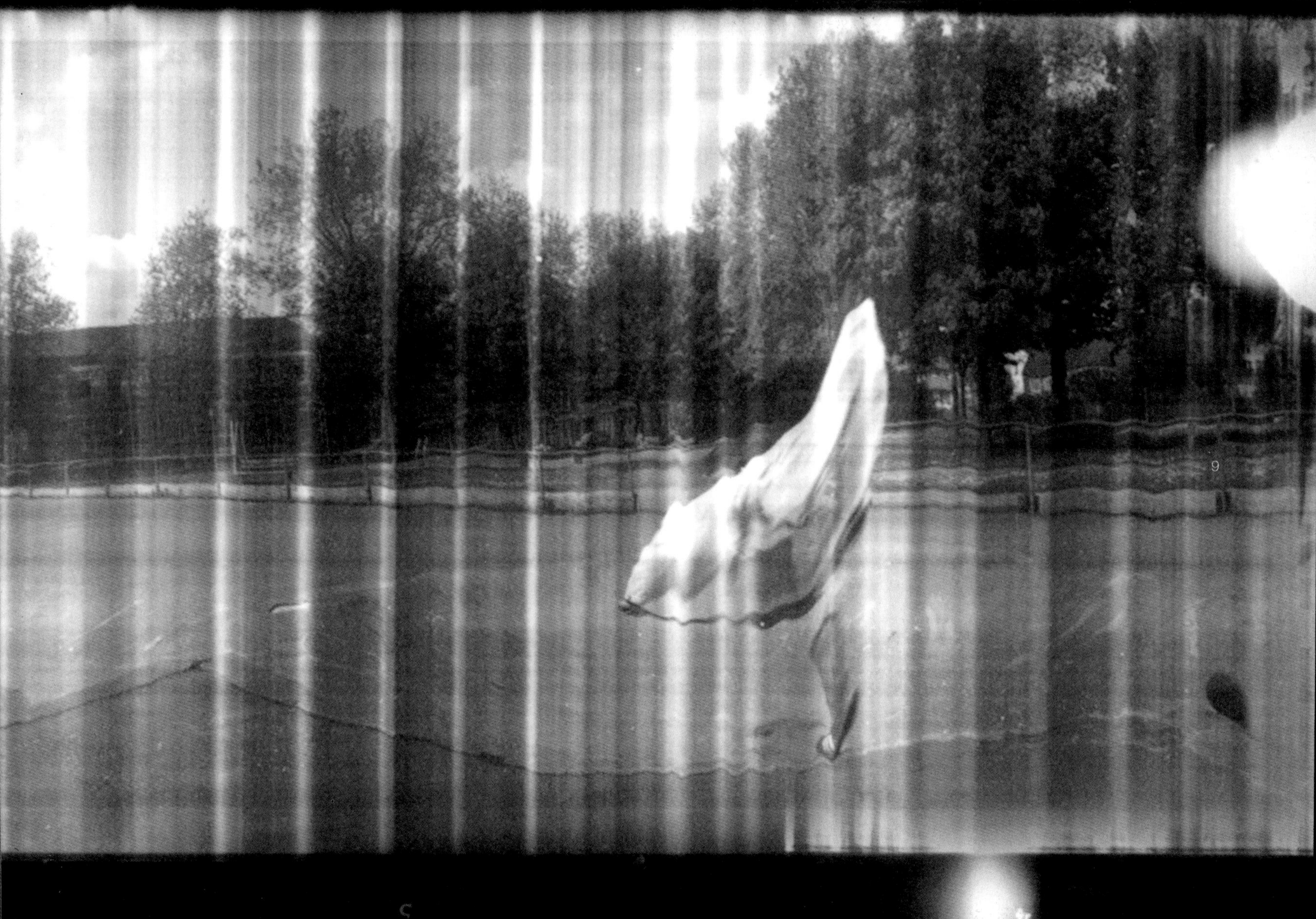

distinguish between science and aesthetics. Even in the contemporary moment of digital proliferation his work takes us back to the fundamentals of a photographic art which furnishes us with new ways of seeing our commonplace world, new ways of making perception visible. Shaw's aspirations and inspirations are underlined by the context of Time | Motion. His work belongs to a photographic tradition of experimentation that has deployed the camera as both

an instrument of scientific record and of aesthetic exploration. Like Muybridge and Edgerton his practice has demanded an engineer's engagement with the form. From his earliest work Shaw has been designing, building and cannibalizing his own customized camera equipment to enable him to produce unique images of time and space. Muybridge and Edgerton were involved in technical and scientific processes which they clearly 'aesthetized' in attempting to

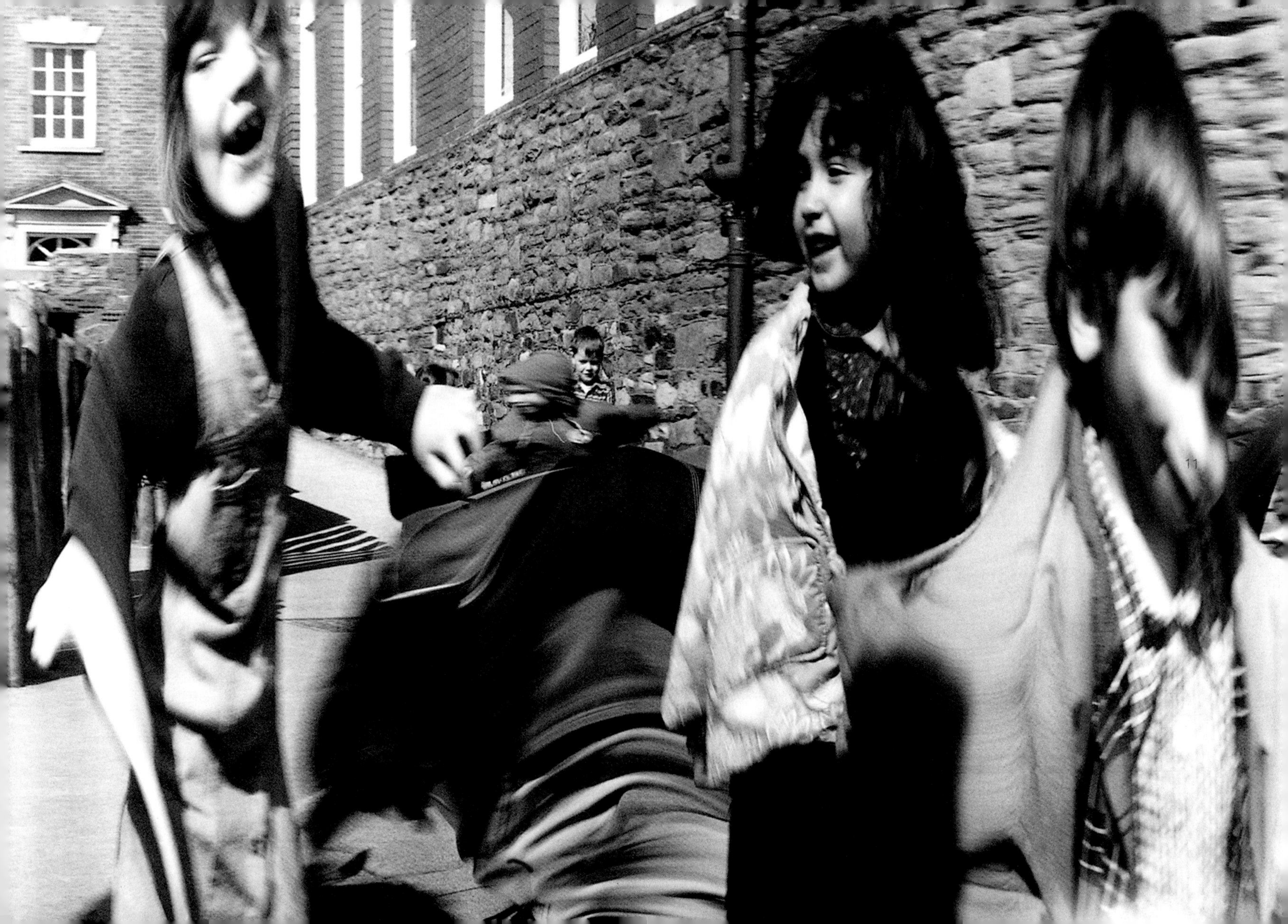

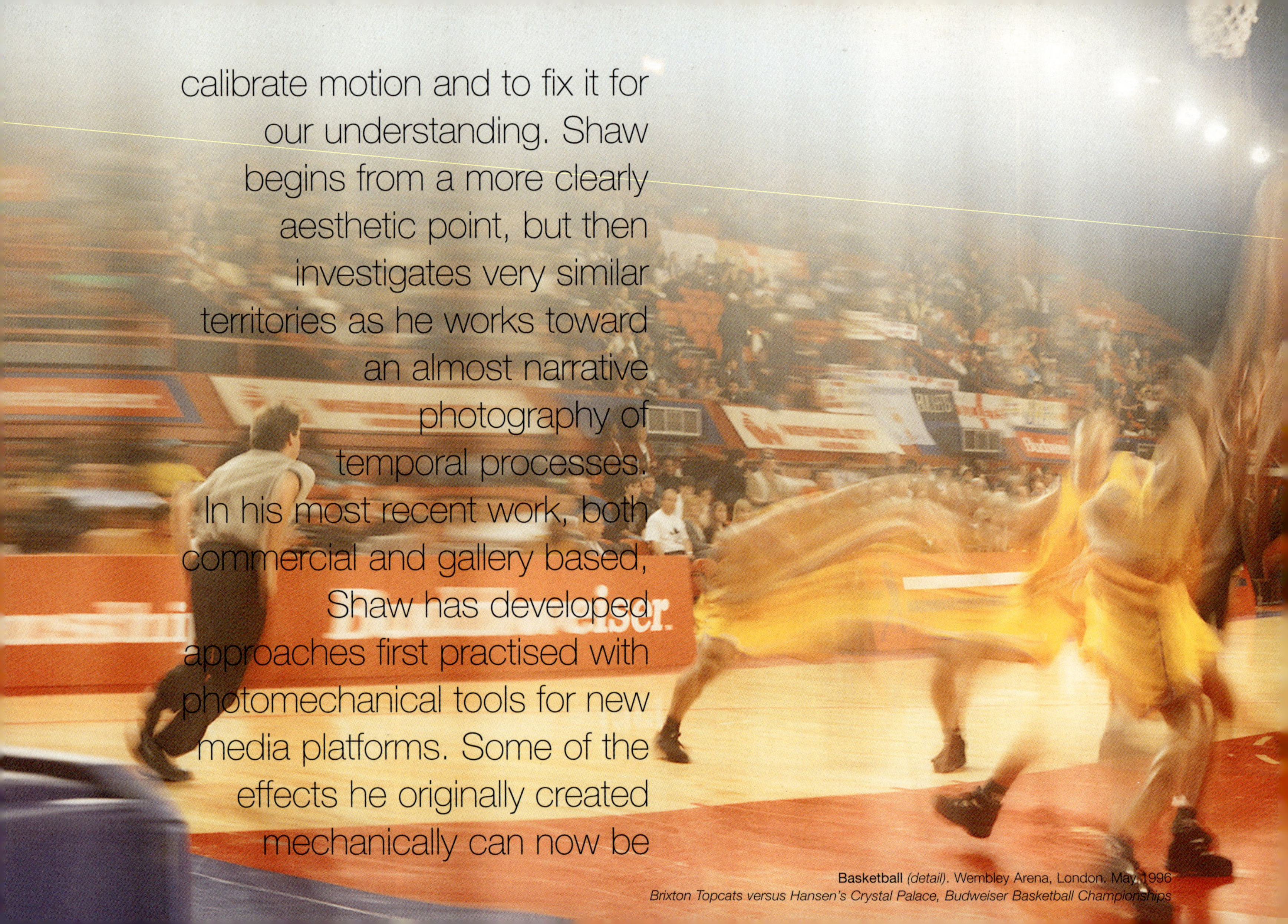

calibrate motion and to fix it for our understanding. Shaw begins from a more clearly aesthetic point, but then investigates very similar territories as he works toward an almost narrative photography of temporal processes. In his most recent work, both commercial and gallery based, Shaw has developed approaches first practised with photomechanical tools for new media platforms. Some of the effects he originally created mechanically can now be

Basketball *(detail)*. Wembley Arena, London. May 1996
Brixton Topcats versus Hansen's Crystal Palace, Budweiser Basketball Championships

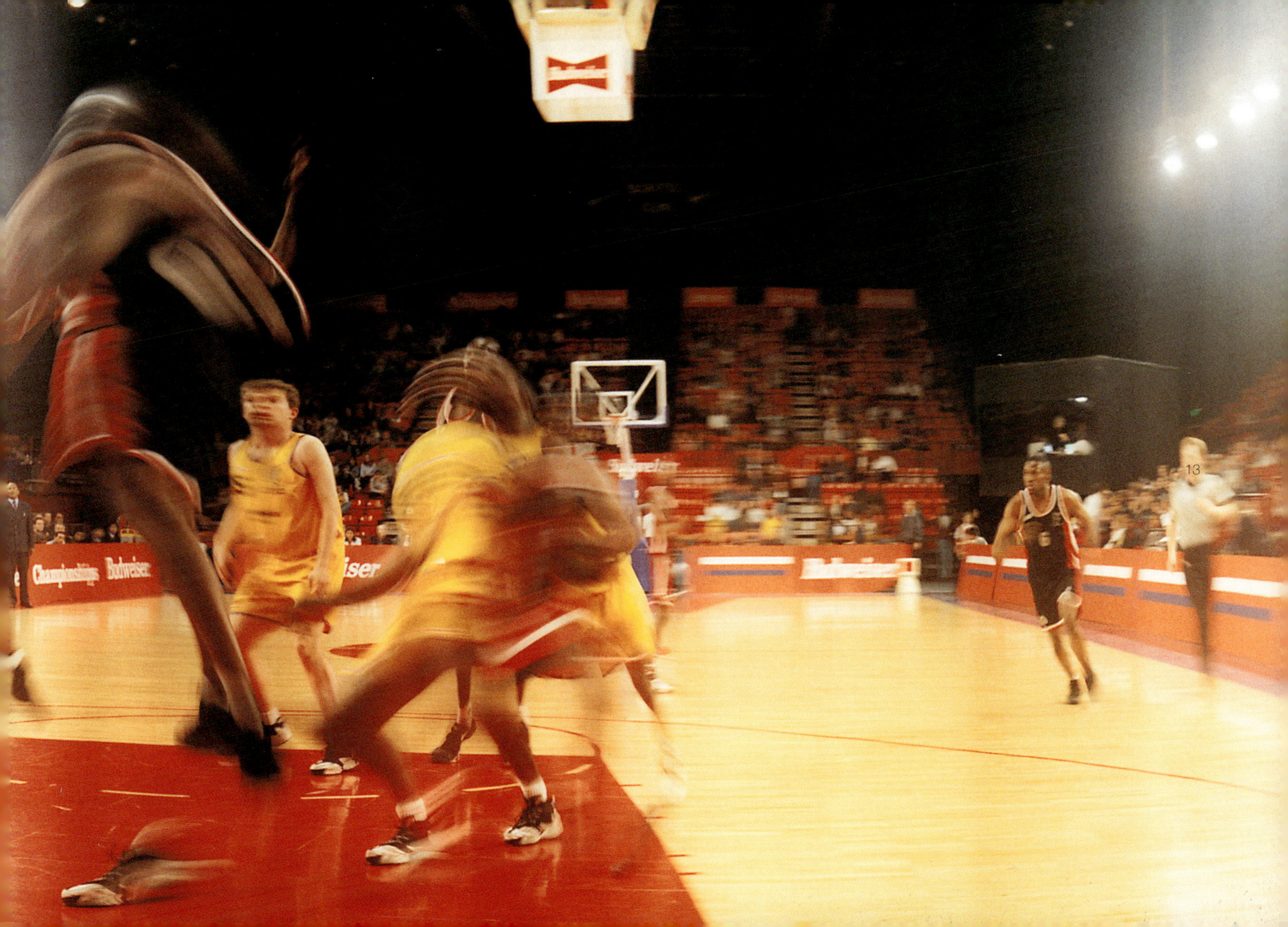
Championships
Budweiser

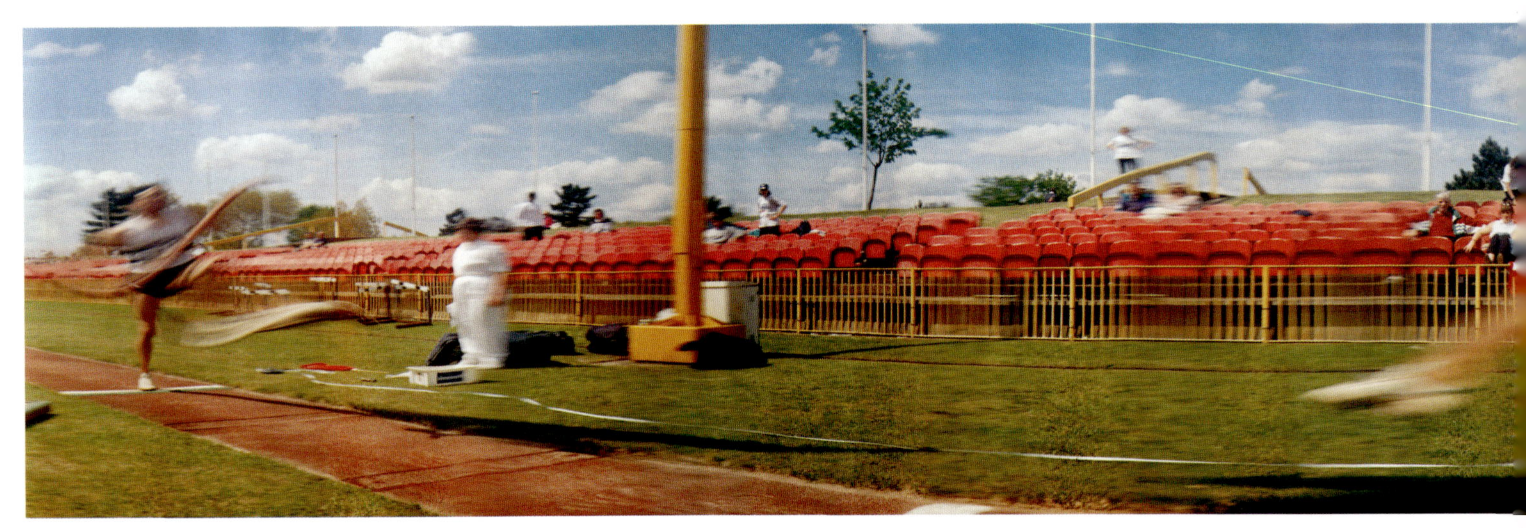

Triple Jump. Alexander Stadium, Birmingham. June 1996

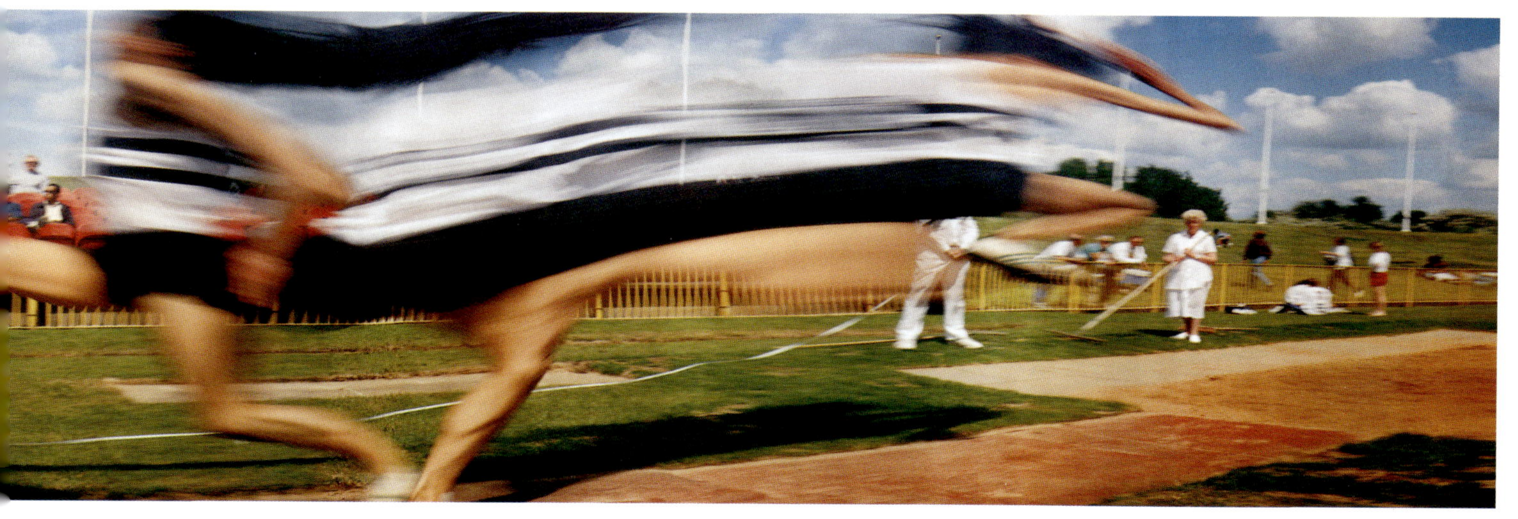

found as part of photo manipulation and digital video software – as such his work can be seen as part of a broader tendency that we might think of as new media archaeologies. That is to say, from the perspective of the possibilities of new media we find ourselves looking back at the history of photomechanical work and reconsidering the potential of the many aesthetic pathways not taken during their development. The digitally created 'bullet time' of 'The Matrix' is prefigured in

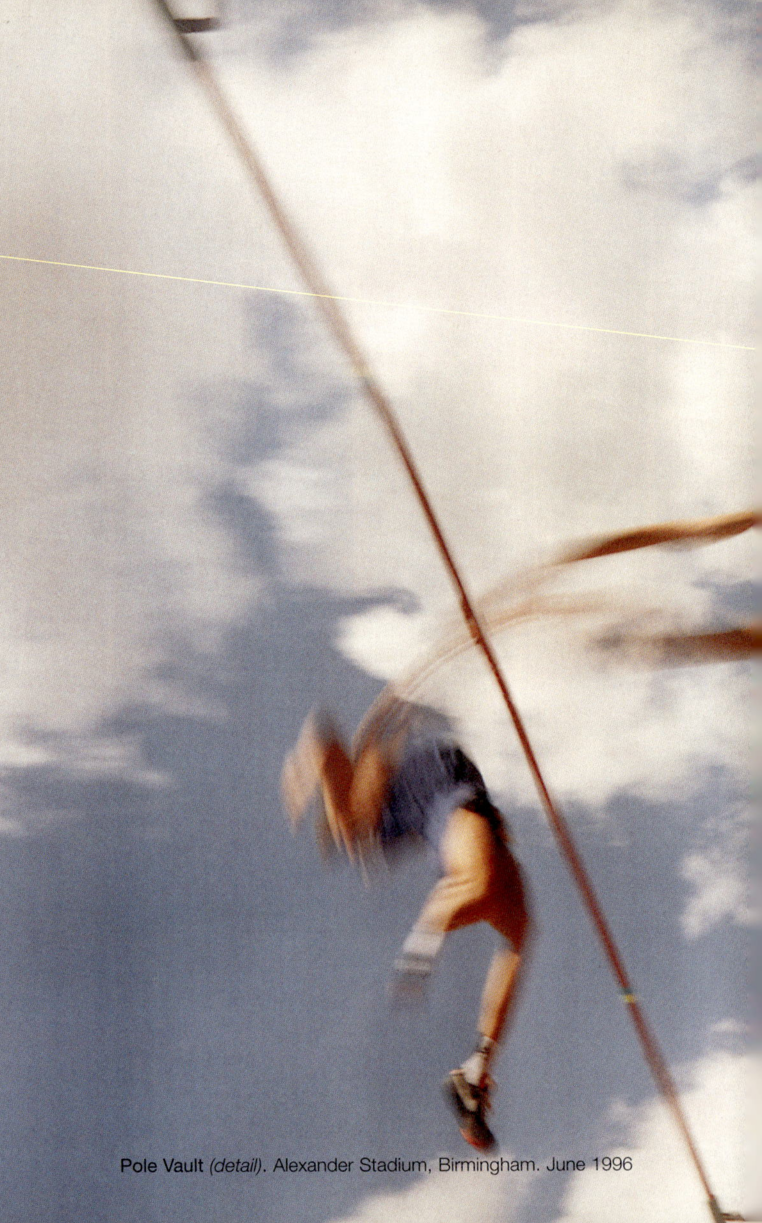

Pole Vault *(detail)*. Alexander Stadium, Birmingham. June 1996

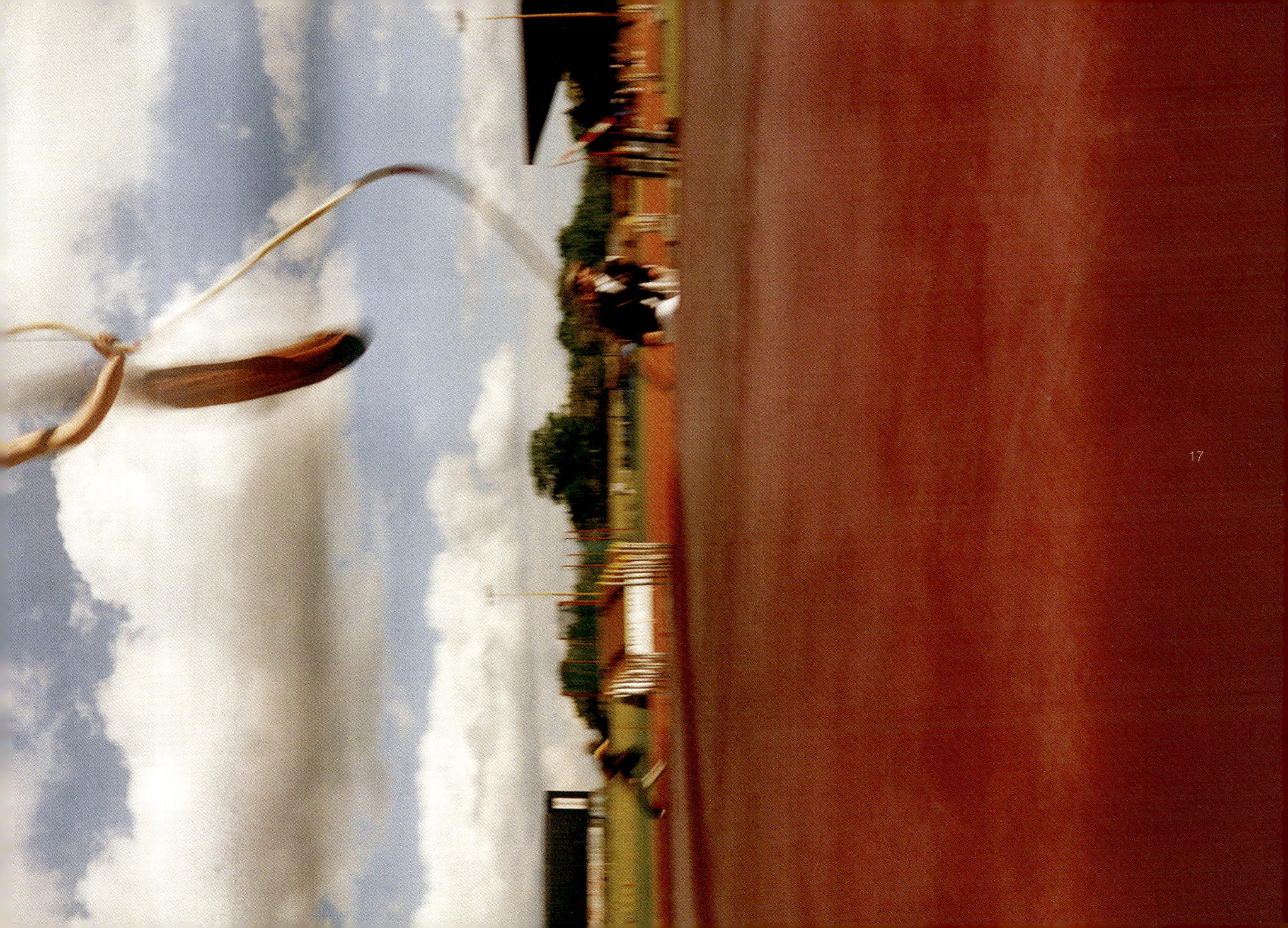

Edgerton's bullet photographs, while Shaw's offer of individual frames for animation by his audience, in the interactive piece, echoes Muybridge's use of a zoopraxiscope to reanimate his images. The work in Time I Motion extends Shaw's fundamental ideas by adding a new element, 'site specificity' would one way of describing it. Shaw's residency at the Museum in Summer 2002 has inspired two works that speak at once of the particular relations of viewing that the

Basketball *(detail)*. Wembley Arena, London. May 1996
London Towers versus Manchester Giants, Budweiser Basketball Championships

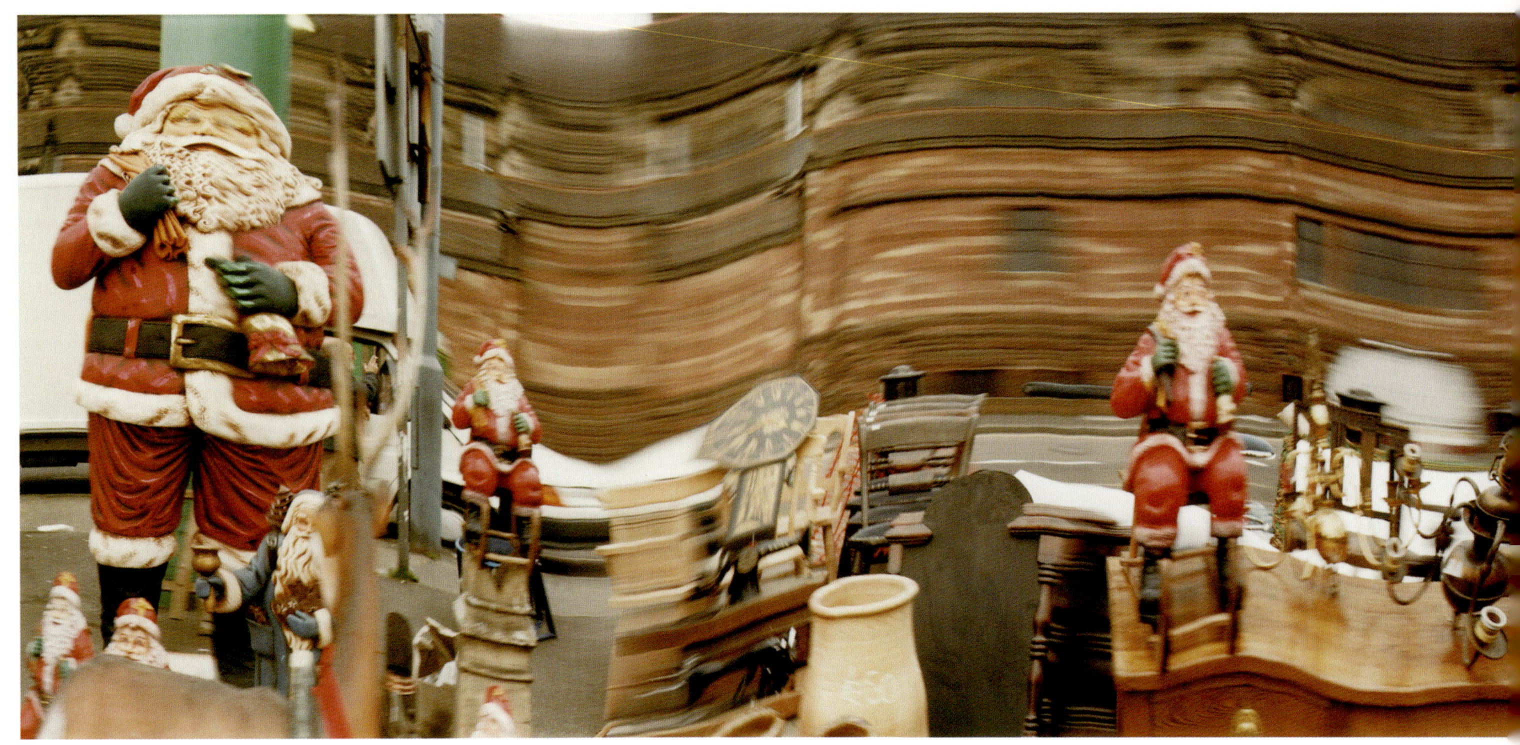

Father Christmas. Bull Ring, Birmingham. 1999

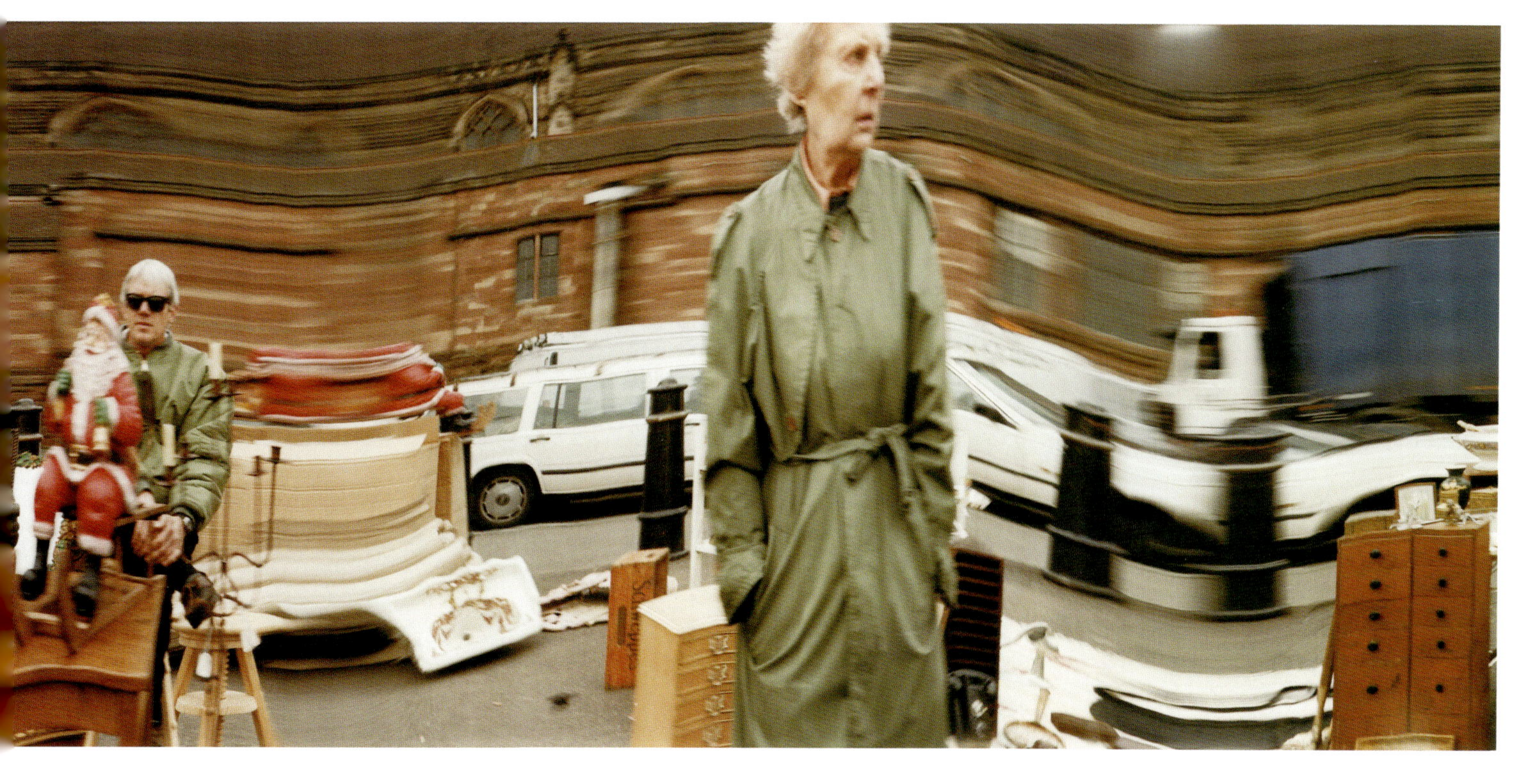

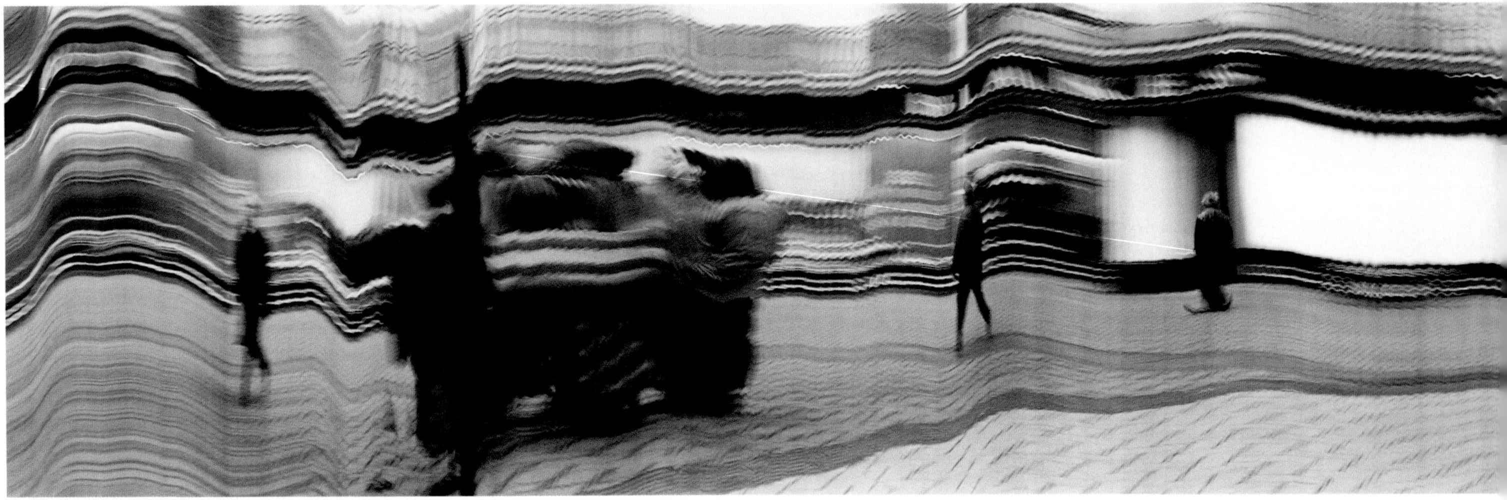

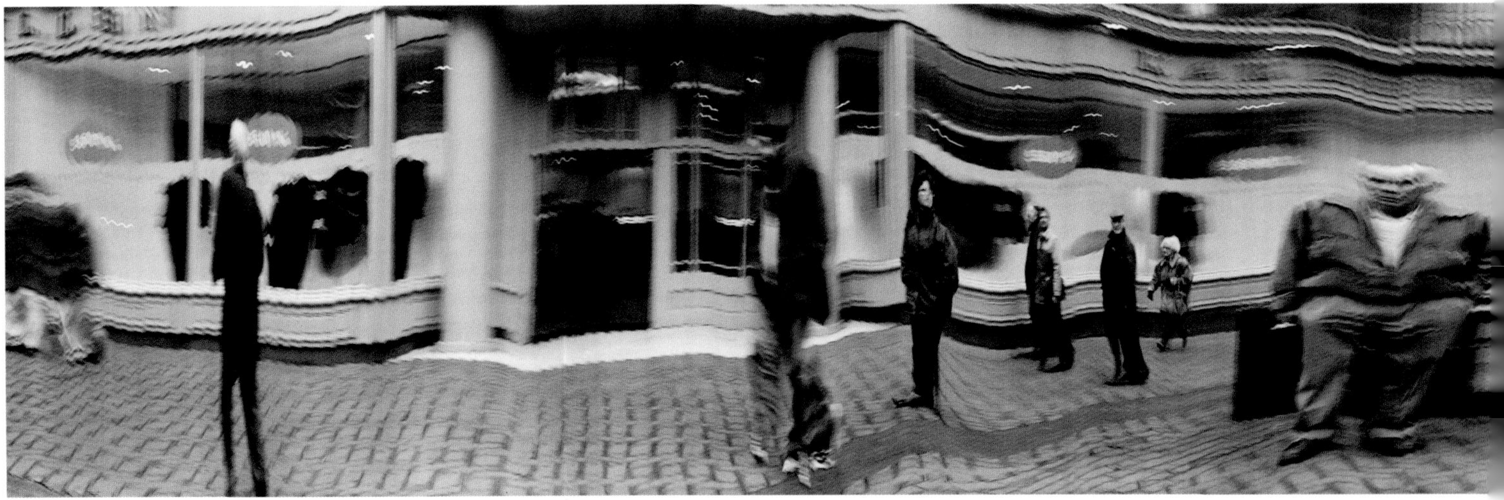

New Street. Birmingham. 1997

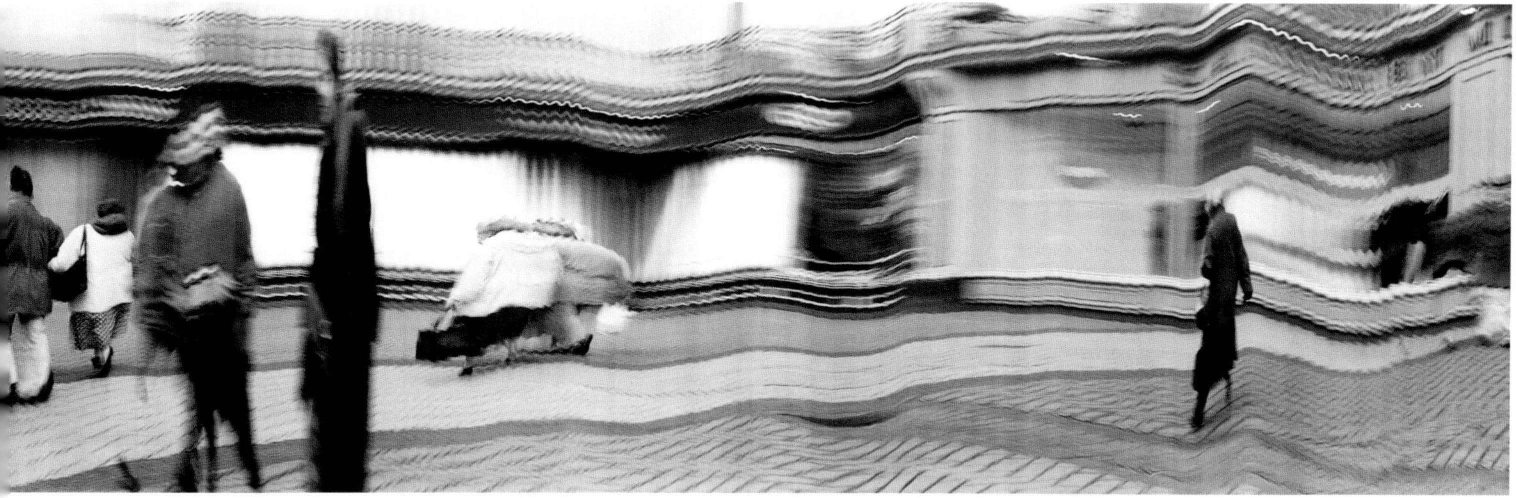

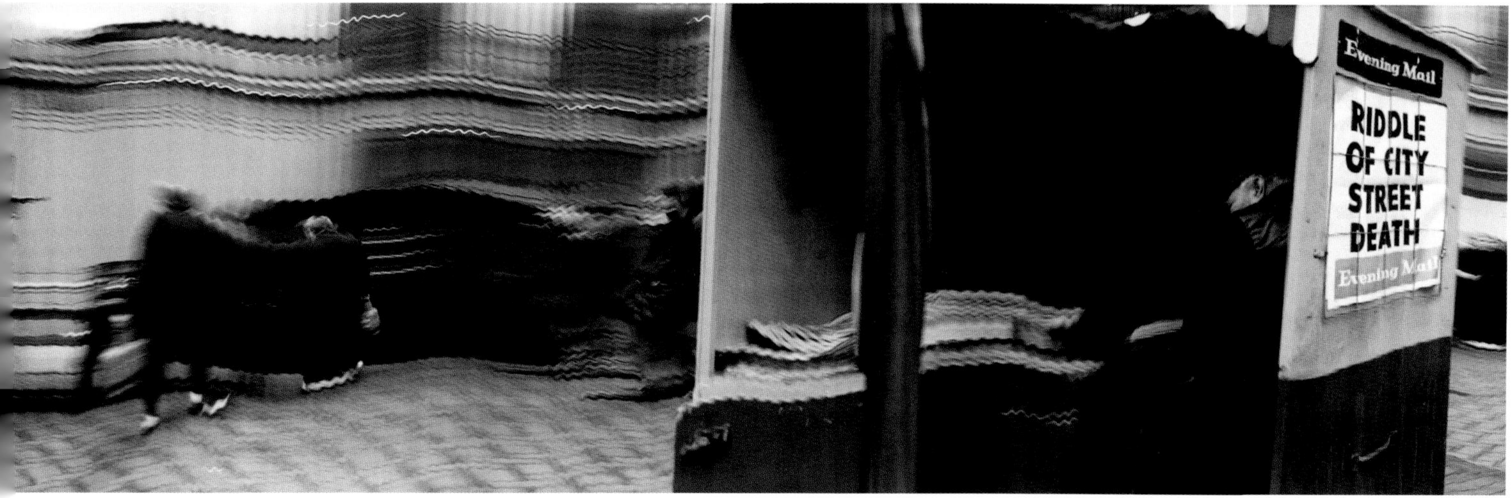
Evening Mail
RIDDLE
OF CITY
STREET
DEATH
Evening Mail

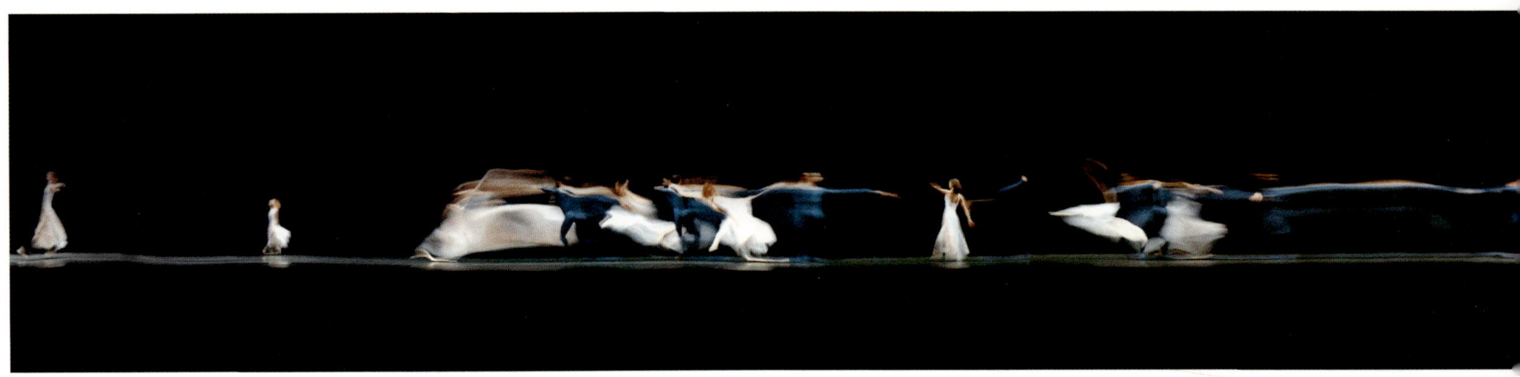

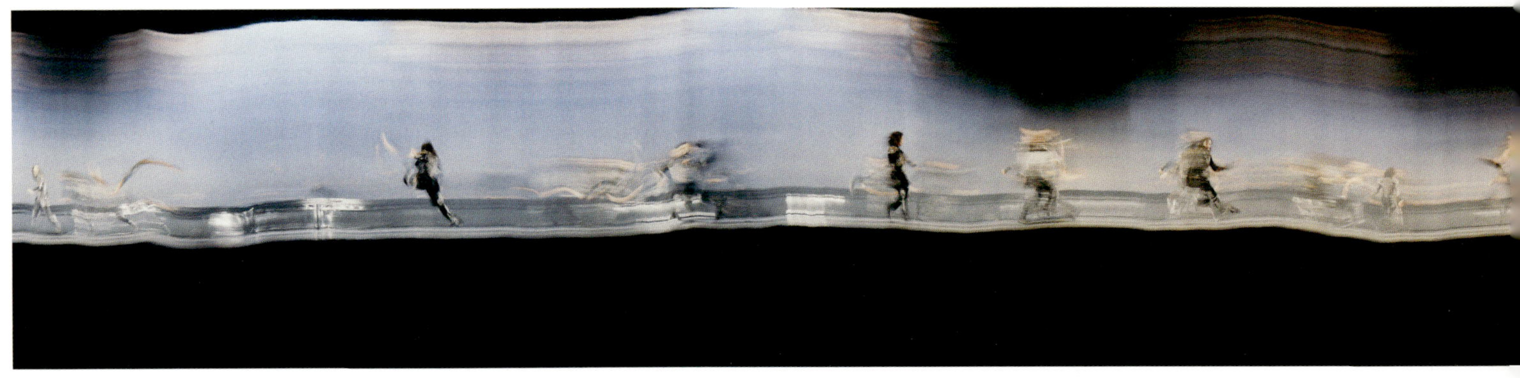

Serenade and Edward II *(respectively)*. Birmingham Hippodrome, Birmingham. 1997
Birmingham Royal Ballet. 'Kinematographs - Explorations of Time, Movement and the Still Image', solo exhibition at F-Stop Media Station, Bath 1998

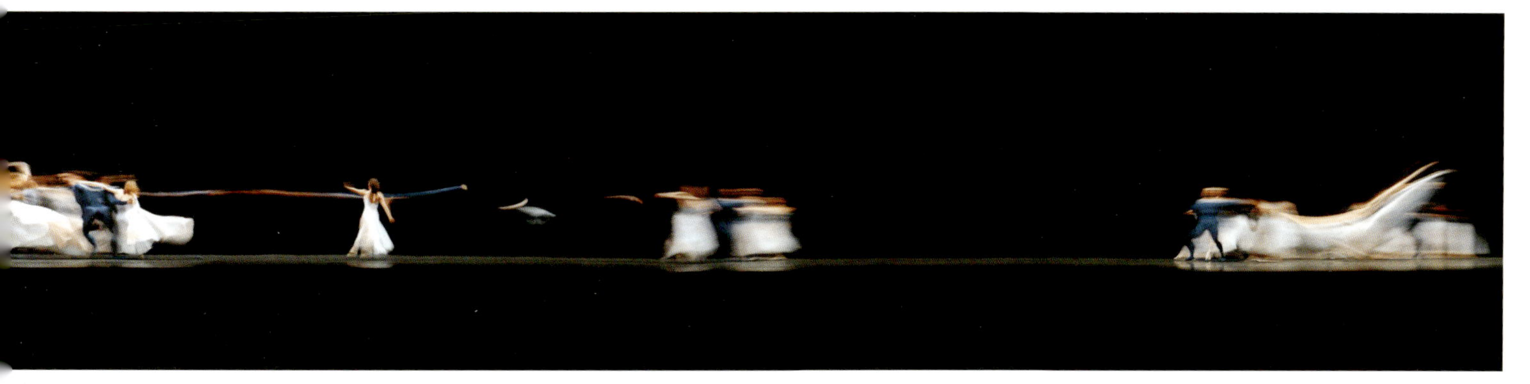

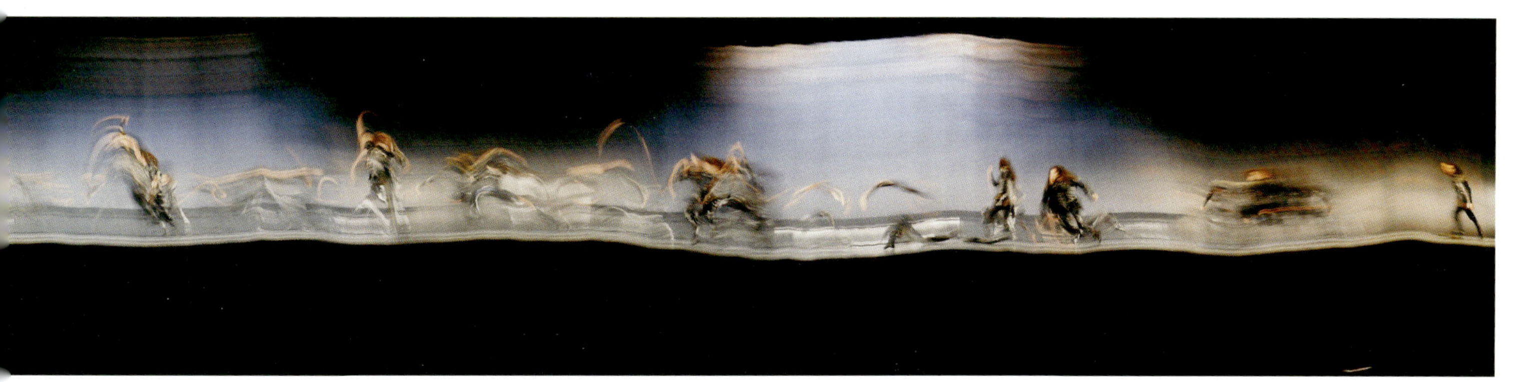

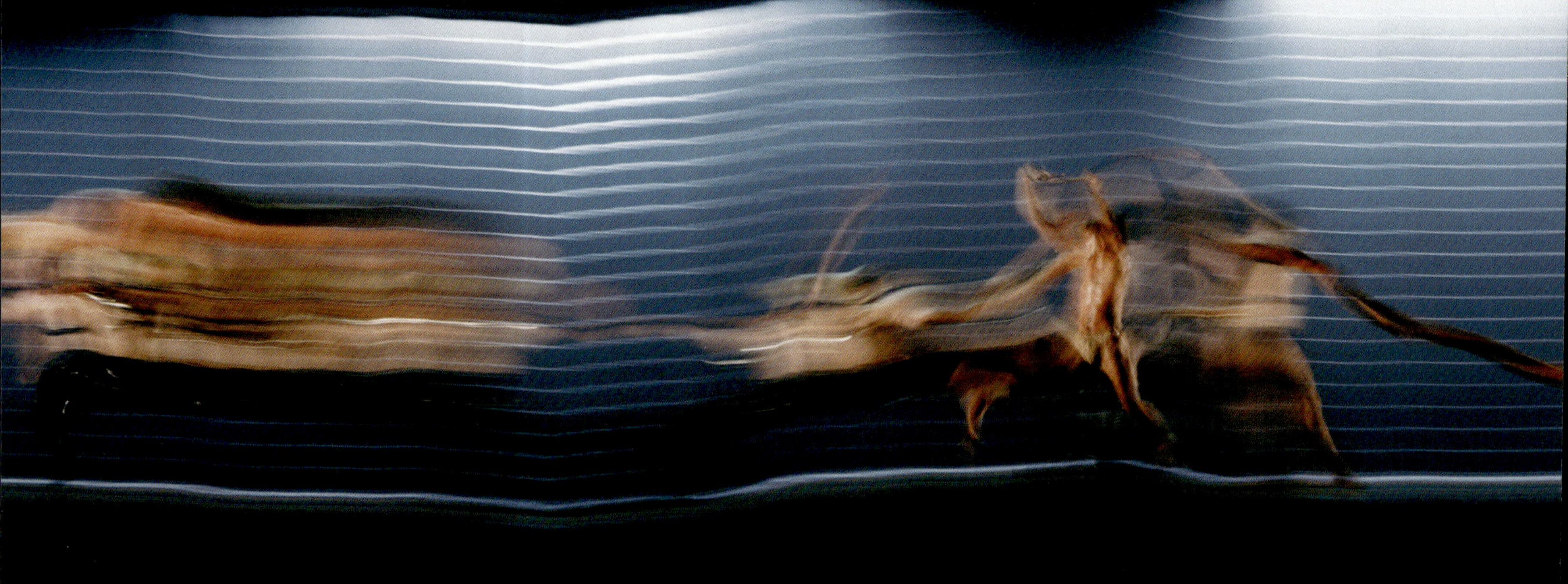

Edward II *(detail)*. Birmingham Hippodrome, Birmingham. 1997
Birmingham Royal Ballet. 'Kinematographs - Explorations of Time, Movement and the Still Image', solo exhibition at F-Stop Media Station, Bath 1998

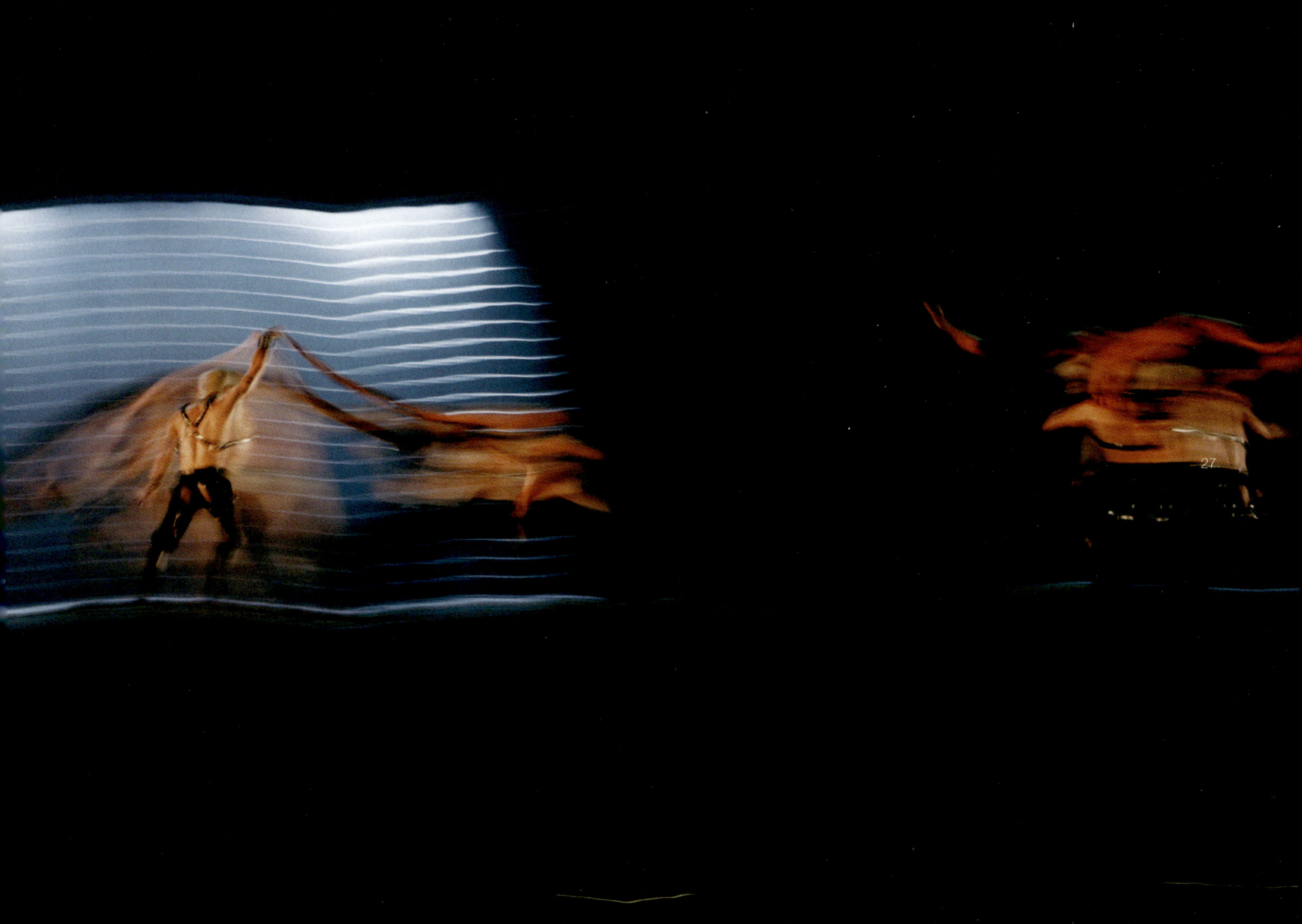

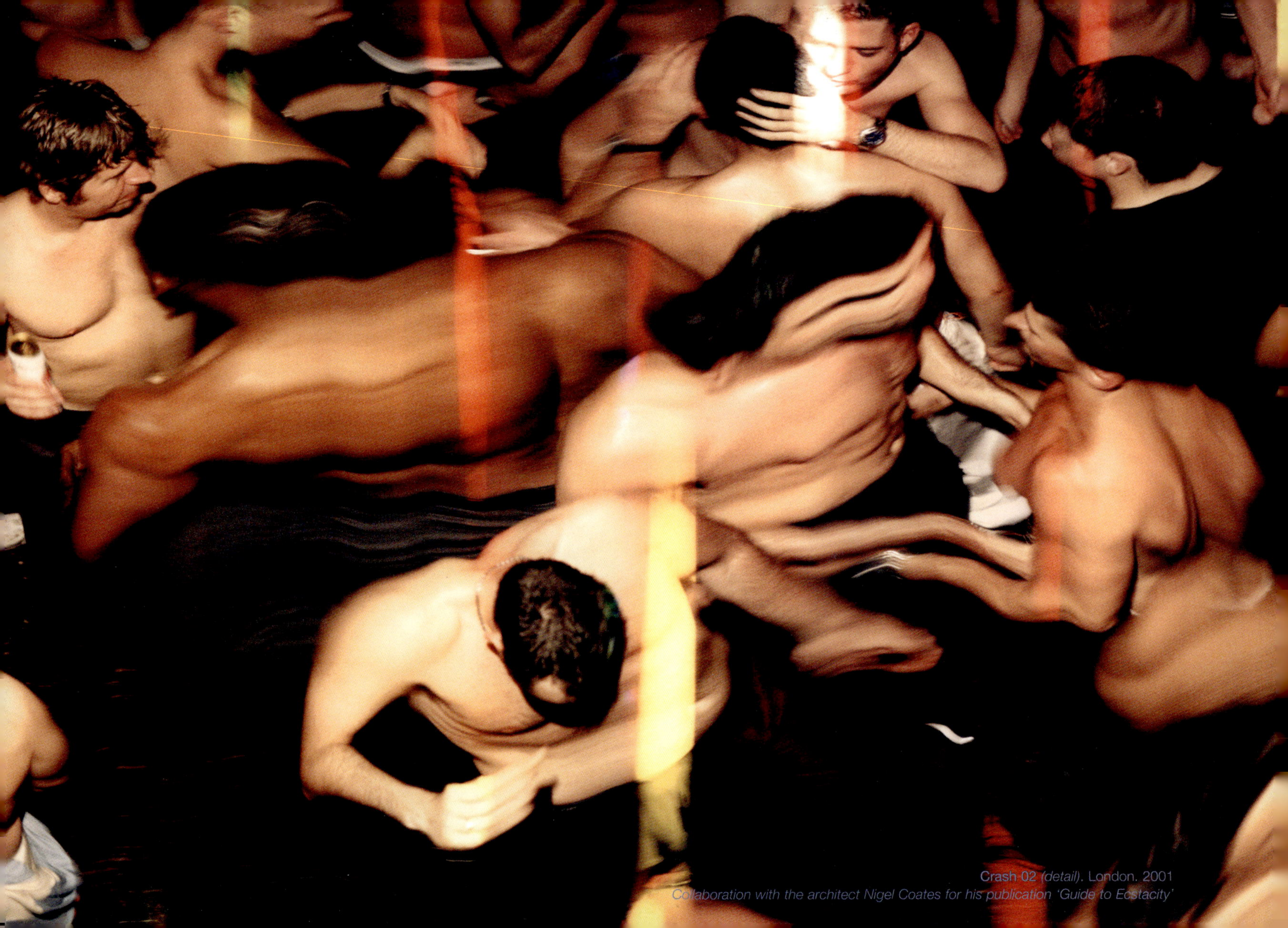

Crash 02 *(detail)*. London. 2001
Collaboration with the architect Nigel Coates for his publication 'Guide to Ecstacity'

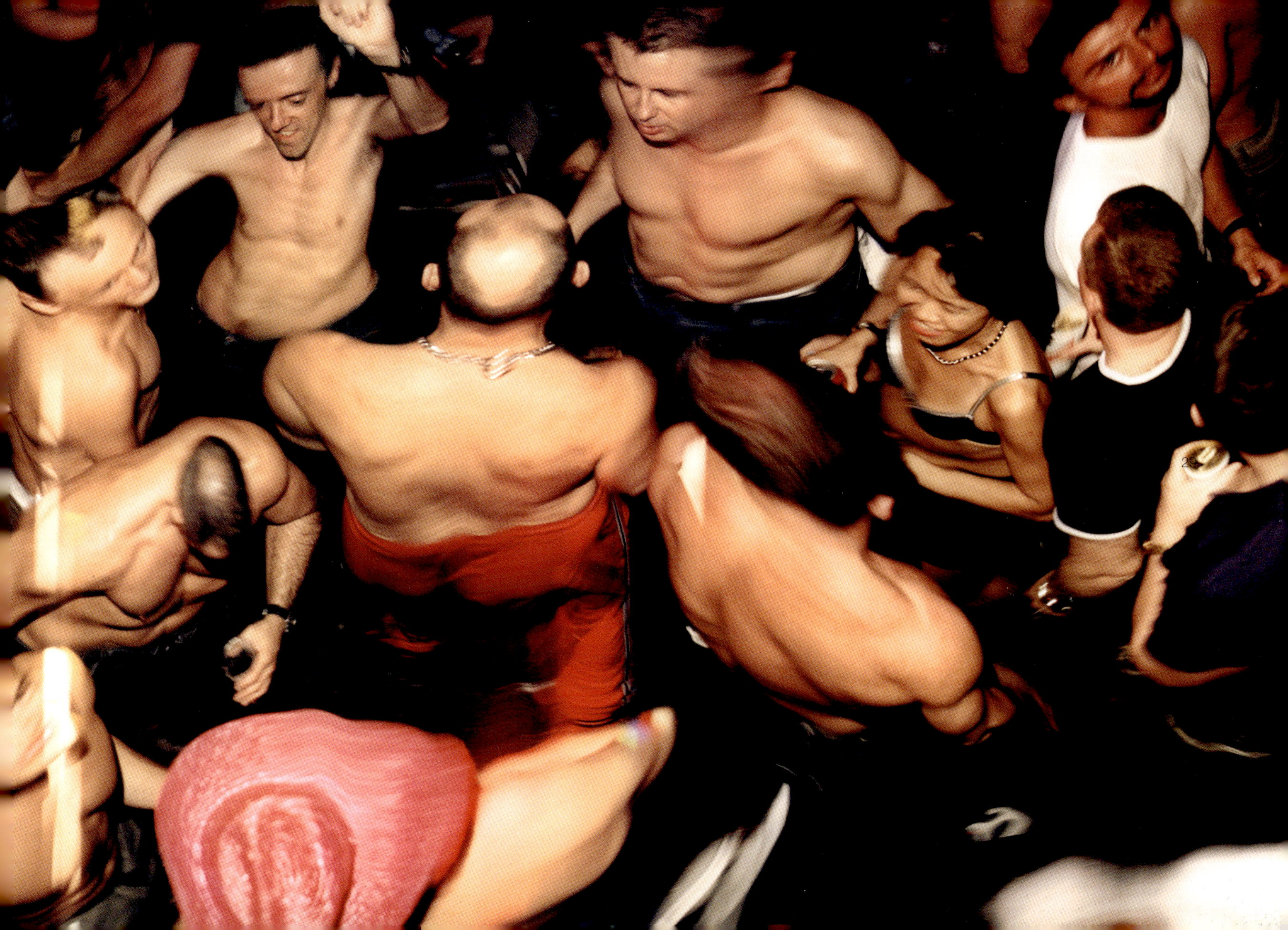

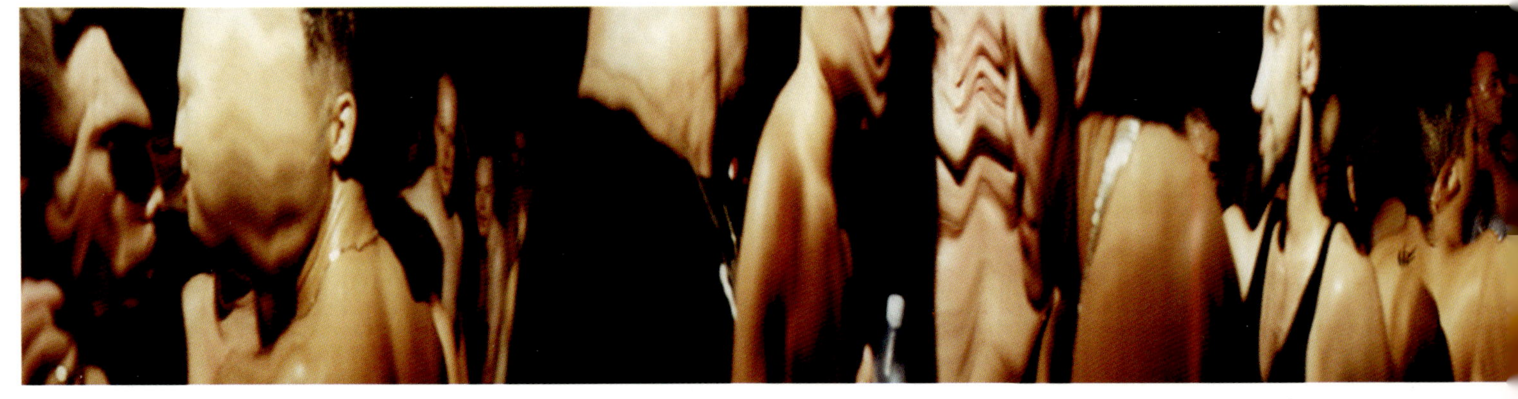

Crash Close-up. London. 2001
Collaboration with the architect Nigel Coates for his publication 'Guide to Ecstacity'

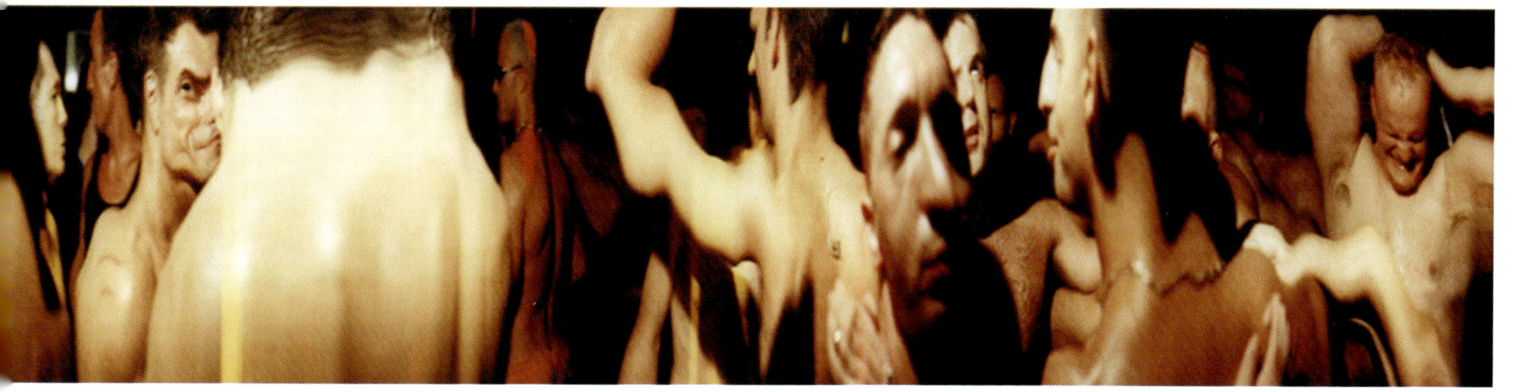

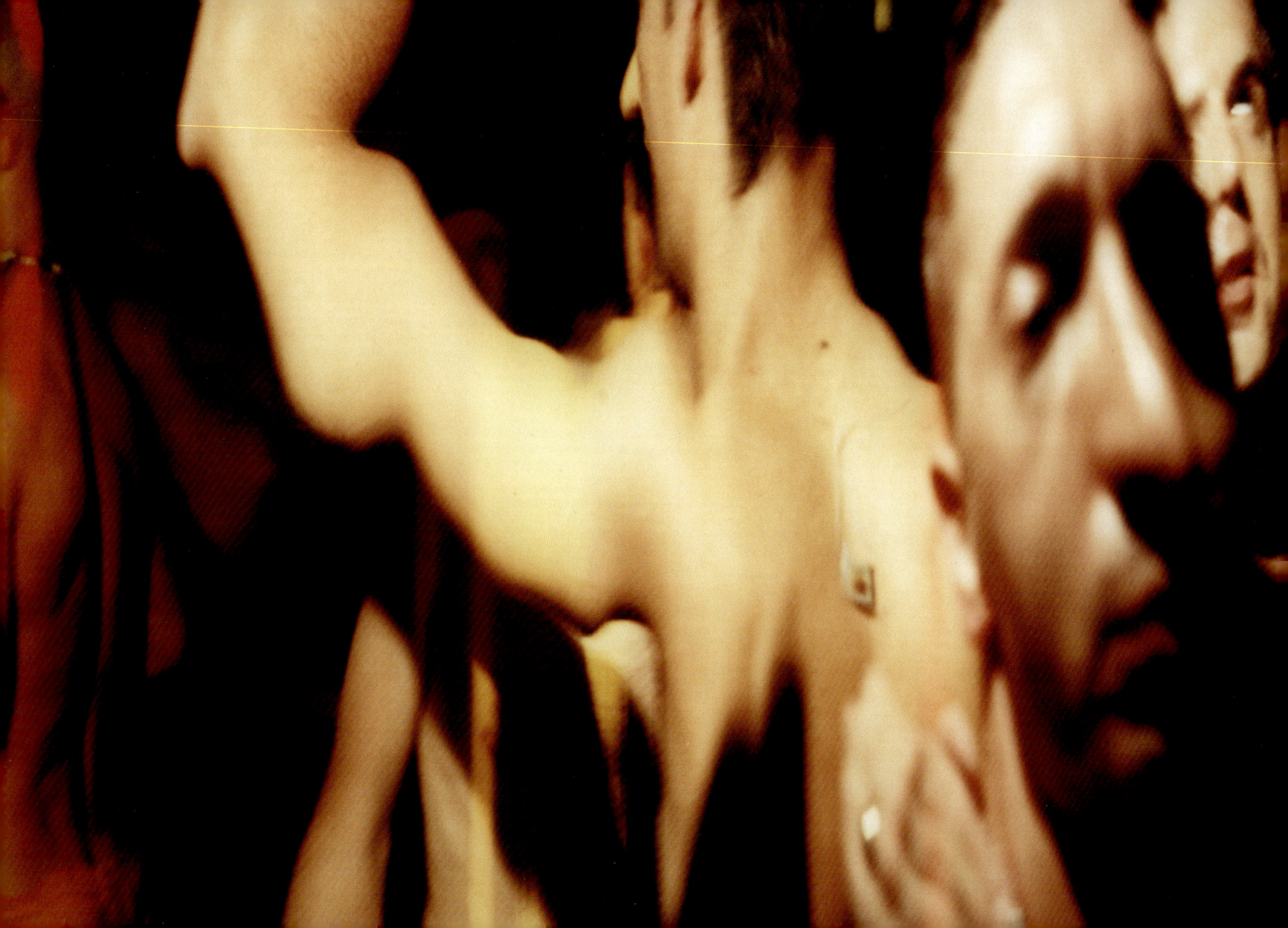

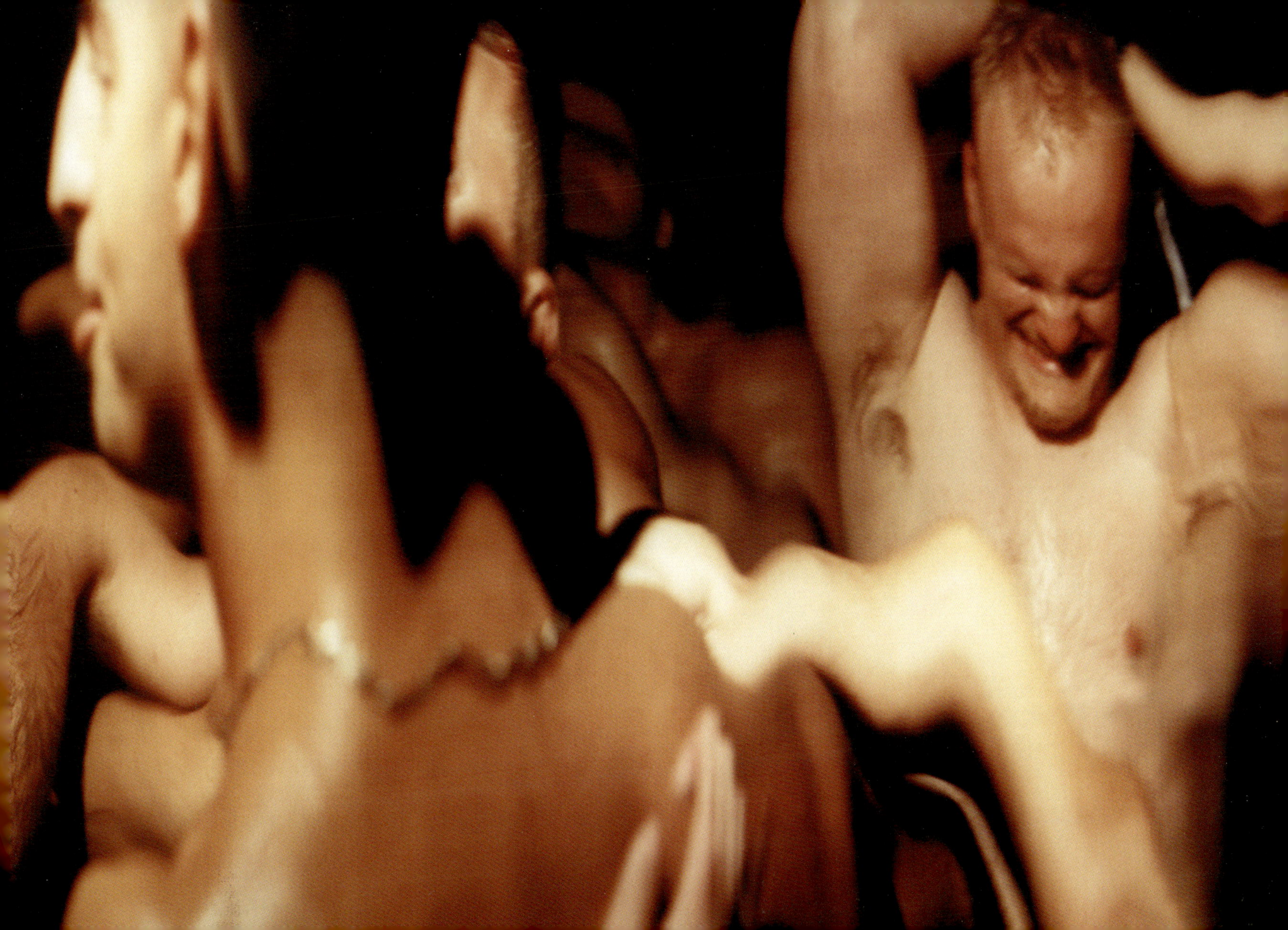

space produces as well as a continuing concern with time and space. Here Shaw's work begins to acknowledge and reciprocate our own spectatorship. 'Gallery 13' is based upon work undertaken during Shaw's residency in which many Museum visitors were photographed in situ and then contacted with a request to participate in Shaw's experiment. Assembled and posed in ways that recalled the original documentation they collaborated with Shaw and his five assistants in **re-presenting themselves for the final 14 metre tracking shot in which the motor that drove the dolly and the camera drive were locked together. The lifesize image, the biggest print ever to be exhibited in the Museum, is like a magic mirror that reflects the past, spectators in a gallery looking at art on the wall, at an opening perhaps, chatting or just gazing. The print brings the past reality of the Museum spectator into the immediate present and as such**

documents a taken for granted or invisible aspect of the Museum itself. The major signature of his earlier work – the stretched faces or background movement blur – is here reduced to a minor key, more of a hint or idea that is intended to prevent us from experiencing the image as simply naturalistic. The interactive piece installed here formulates a similar set of ideas in so far as Shaw is again working with Museum spectatorship and asking us to participate in his experiment.

Starting from the idea that we are all increasingly sophisticated users and viewers of moving image technologies the piece attempts to return us to their fundamental constituents. Here the mirror effect is replaced by something more akin to surveillance, another kind of self-imaging. During the original residency Shaw created an installation which used an extremely slow shutter speed on the video camera (3fps) to make the moving subject clear and the

Time | Motion Interactive stills. Birmingham Museum and Art Gallery, Birmingham. Summer 2002
Commissioned by Birmingham Museums and Art Gallery and Birmingham Library Services. Funded through the Arts Council of England.

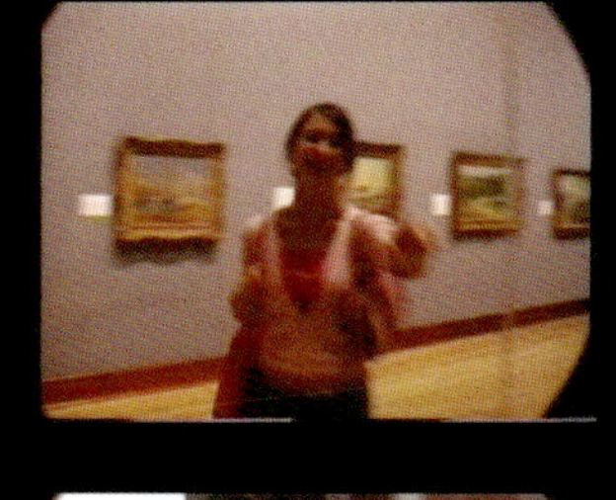
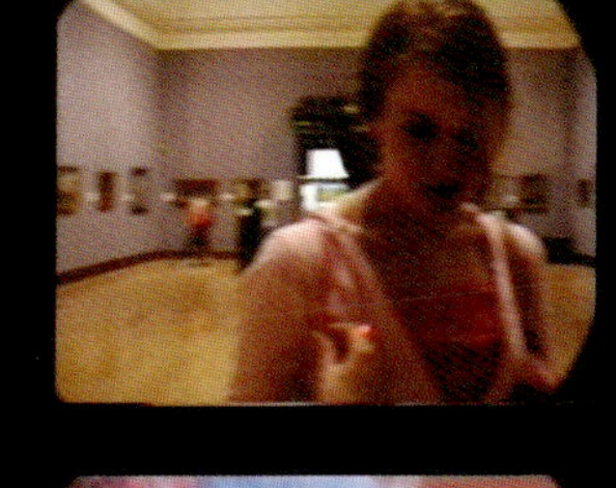
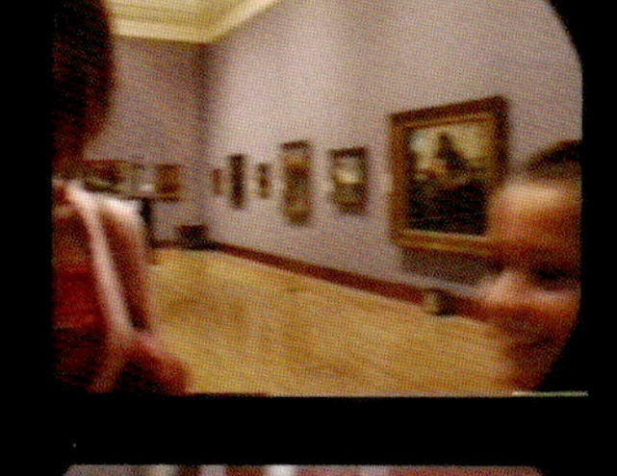
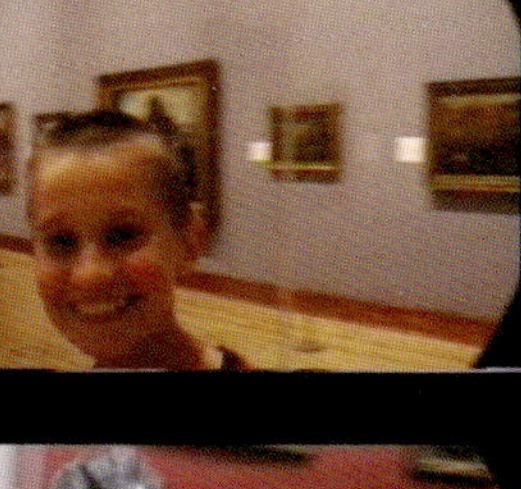
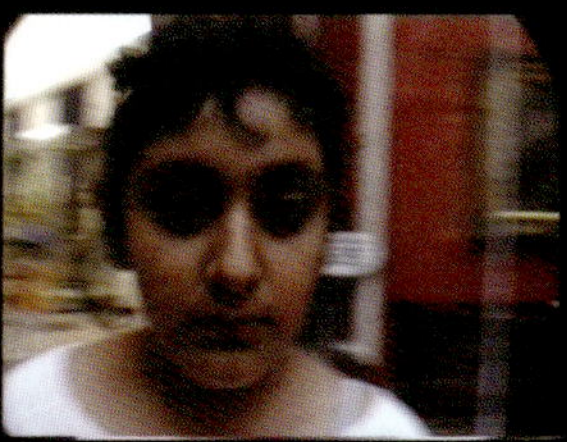
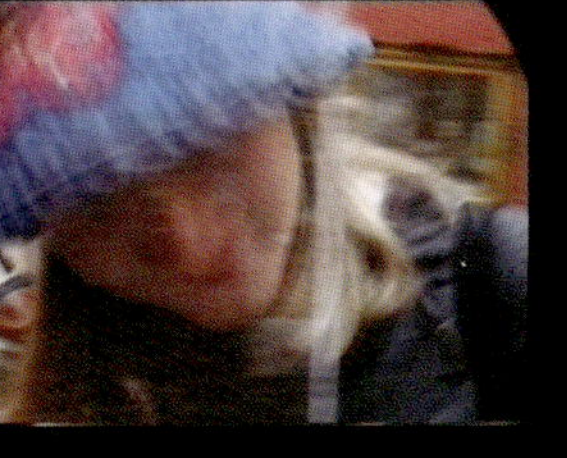
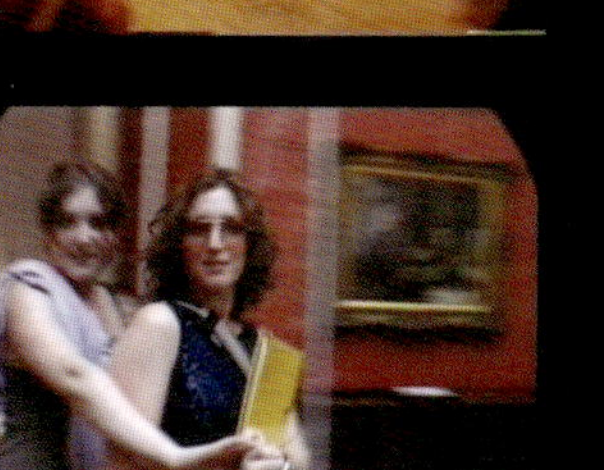
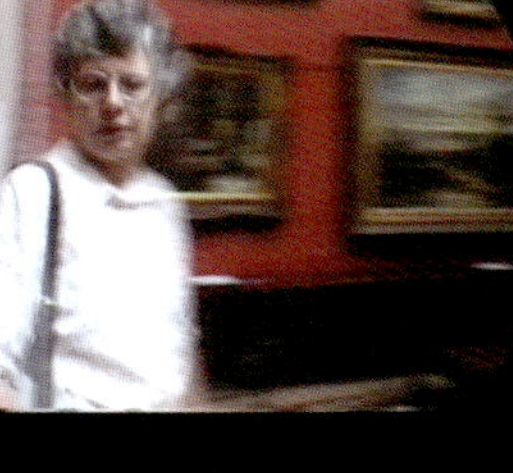
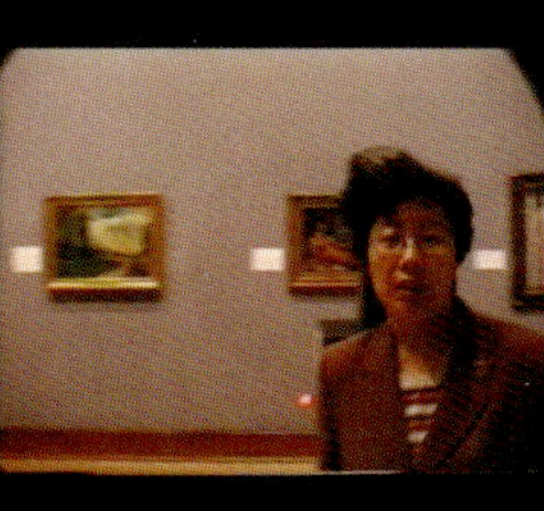
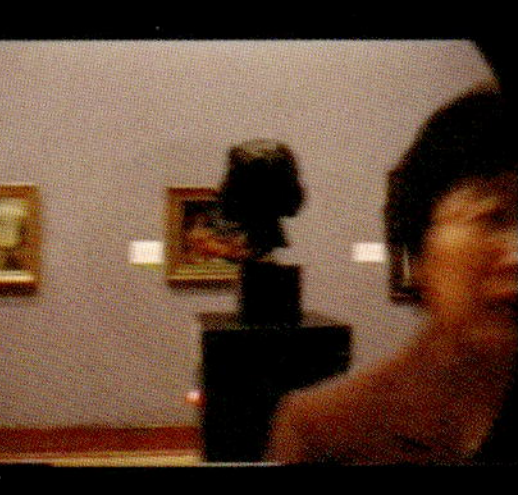
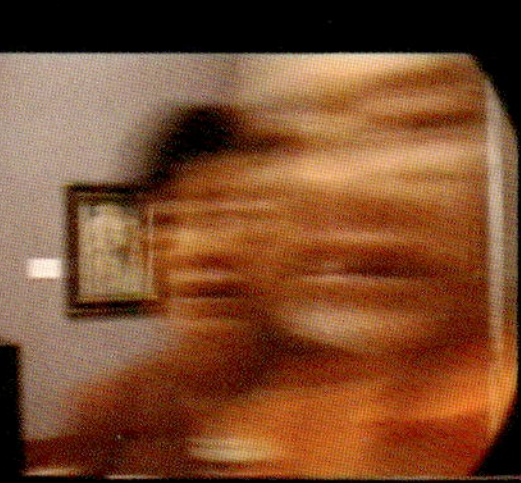
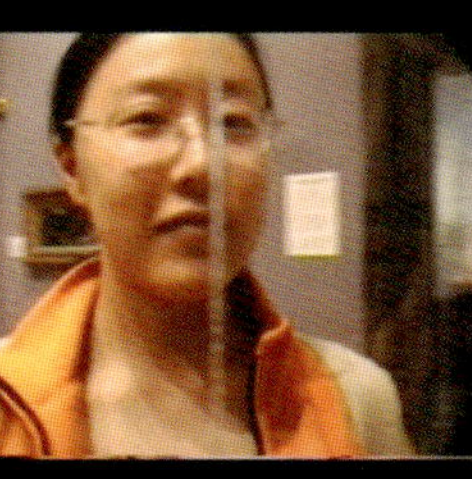

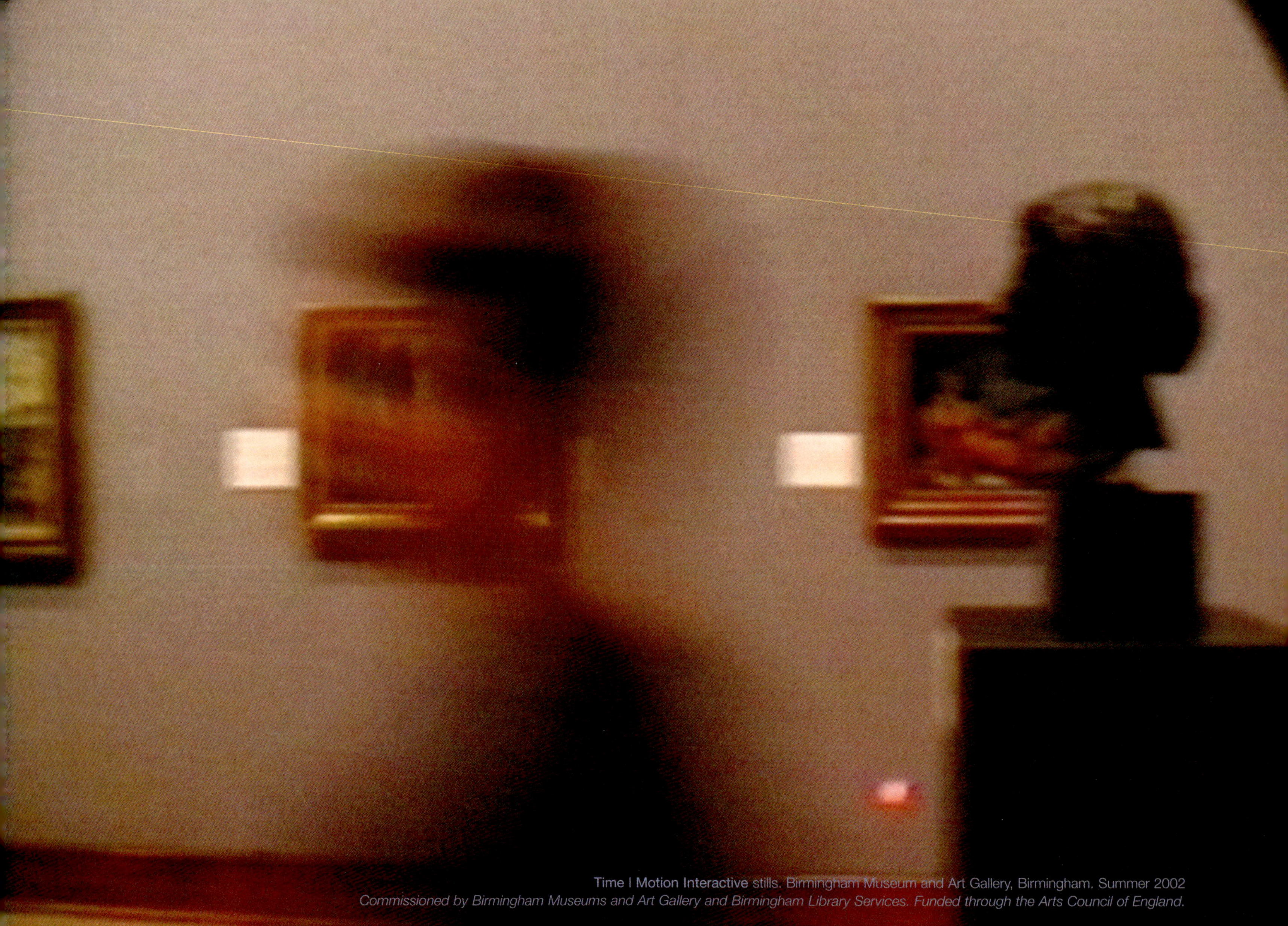

Time | Motion Interactive stills. Birmingham Museum and Art Gallery, Birmingham. Summer 2002
Commissioned by Birmingham Museums and Art Gallery and Birmingham Library Services. Funded through the Arts Council of England.

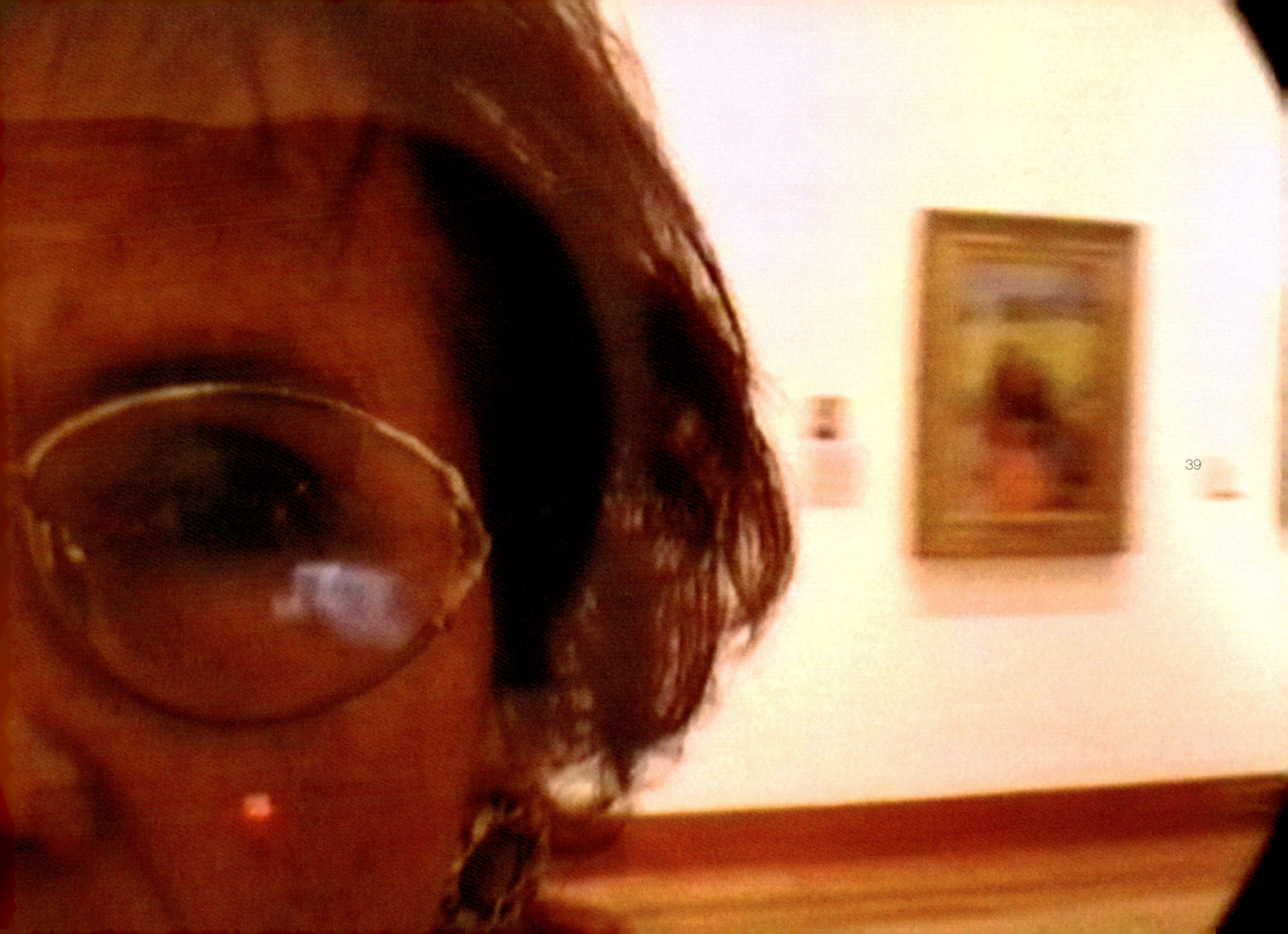

static gallery background a blur, reversing the conventional arrangement. The viewers were drawn into a shuffling dance of capture and evasion in which their own bodies seem to drive the process. This process was however only the beginning of an artwork that is to be created by the users who are now invited to view and to edit the recordings, making new works that again re-present the Museum's past in its present.

Jonathan Shaw is steadily accumulating a distinctive and ground breaking body of work. Its technical accomplishment and its beauty are the product of a disciplined fascination with the relationship between photomechanical reproduction and time. The central issues of his work have remained constant yet he continues to find new and fruitful ways of exploiting them. He is a genuine original.

Jon Dovey

Time | **Motion Interactive** stills. Birmingham Museum and Art Gallery, Birmingham. Summer 2002

Commissioned by Birmingham Museums and Art Gallery and Birmingham Library Services. Funded through the Arts Council of England.

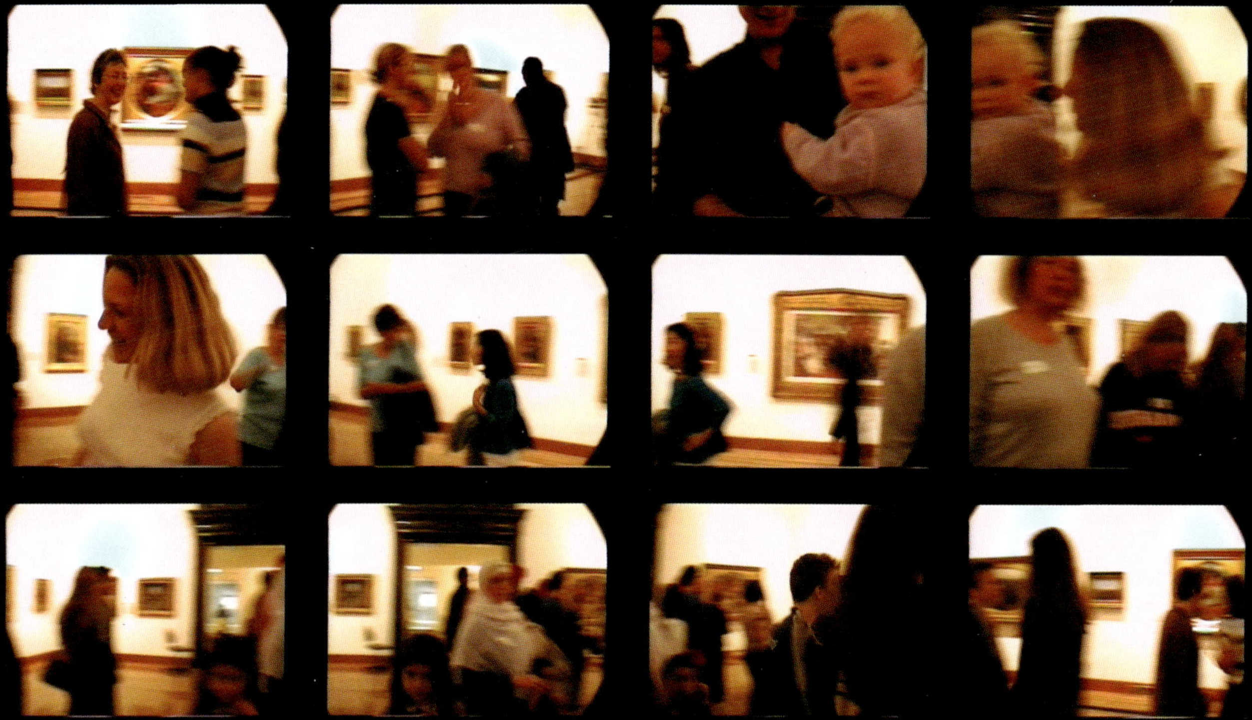

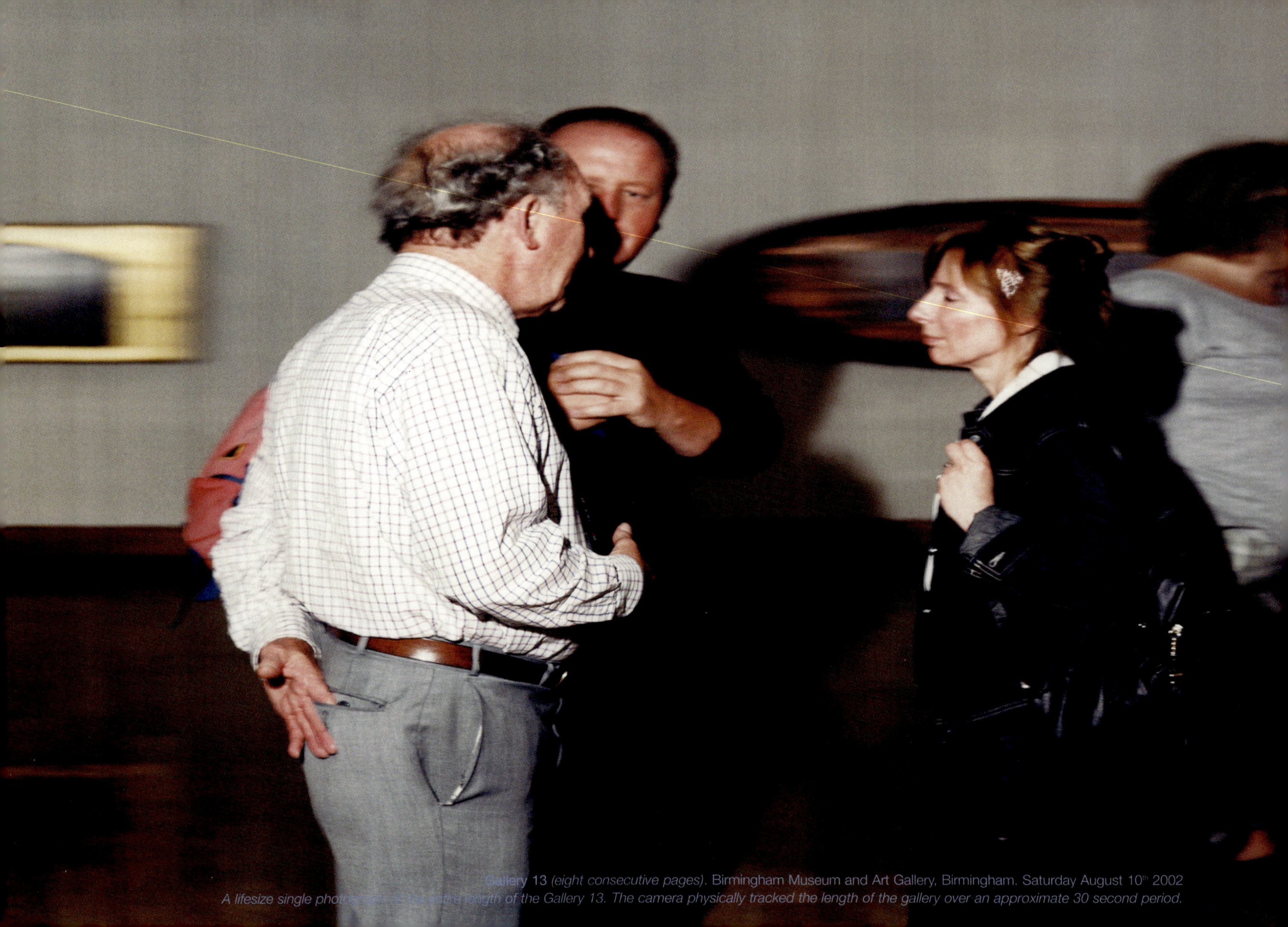

Gallery 13 *(eight consecutive pages)*. Birmingham Museum and Art Gallery, Birmingham. Saturday August 10th 2002
A lifesize single photograph of the entire length of the Gallery 13. The camera physically tracked the length of the gallery over an approximate 30 second period.

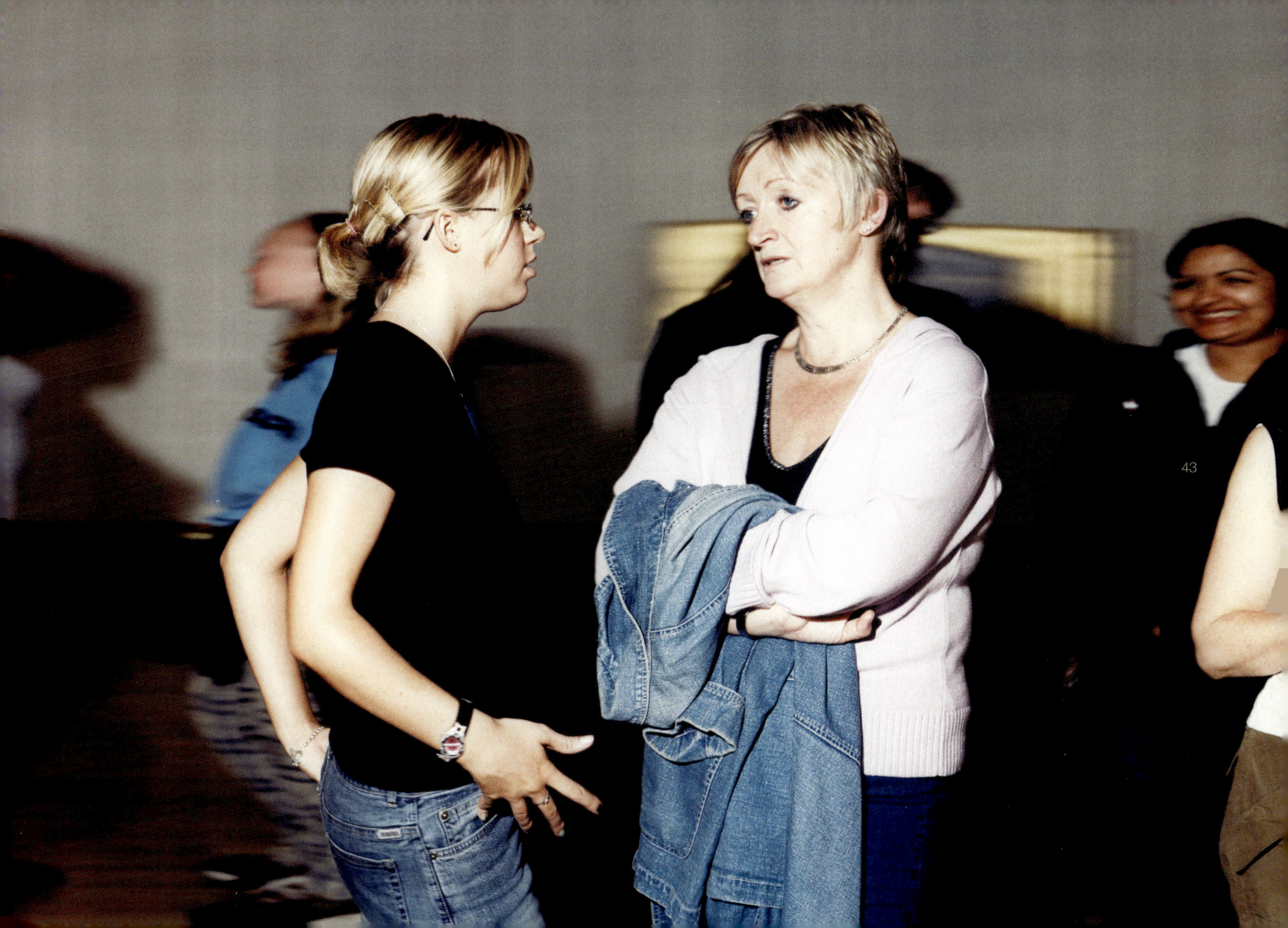

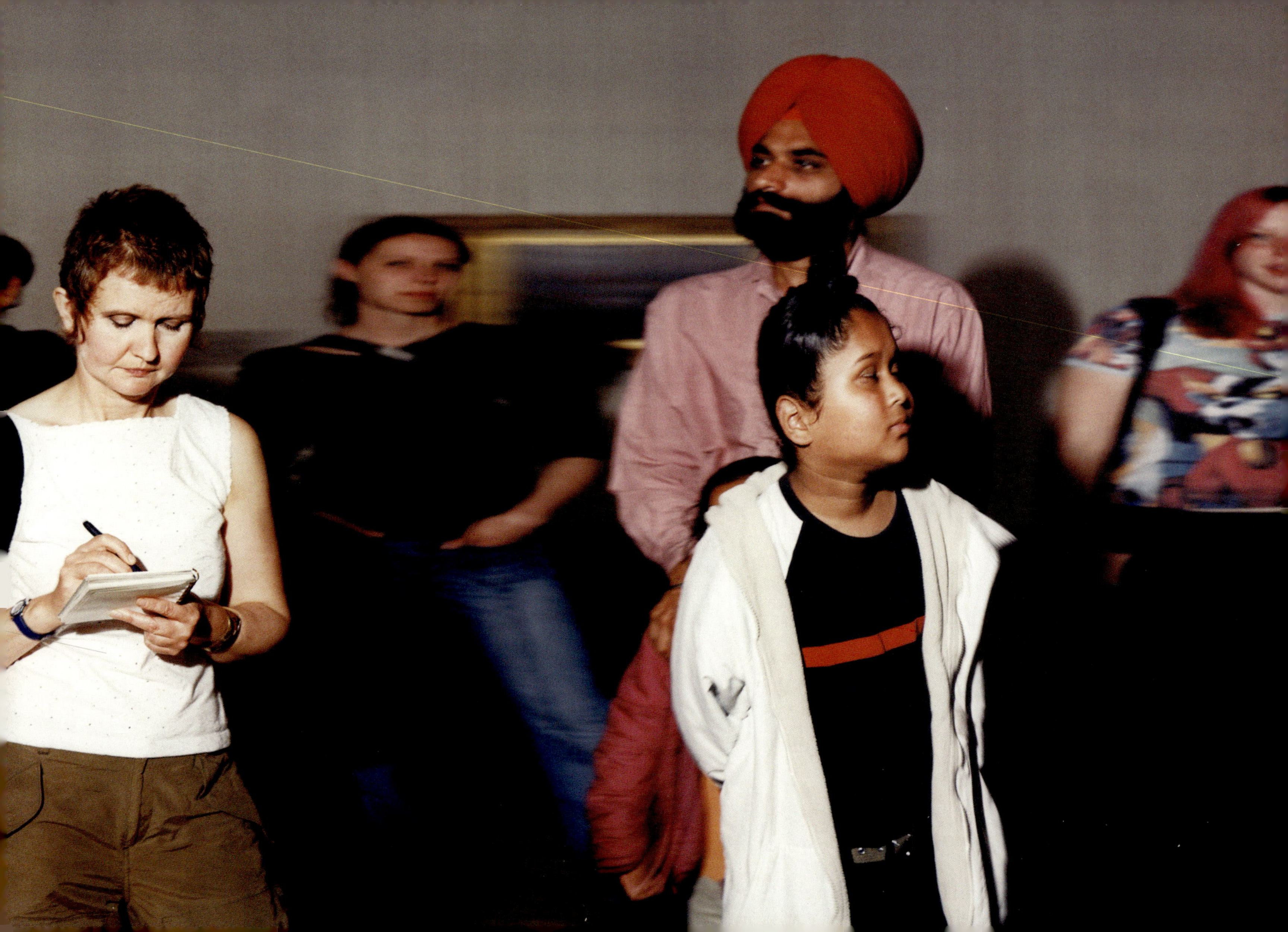

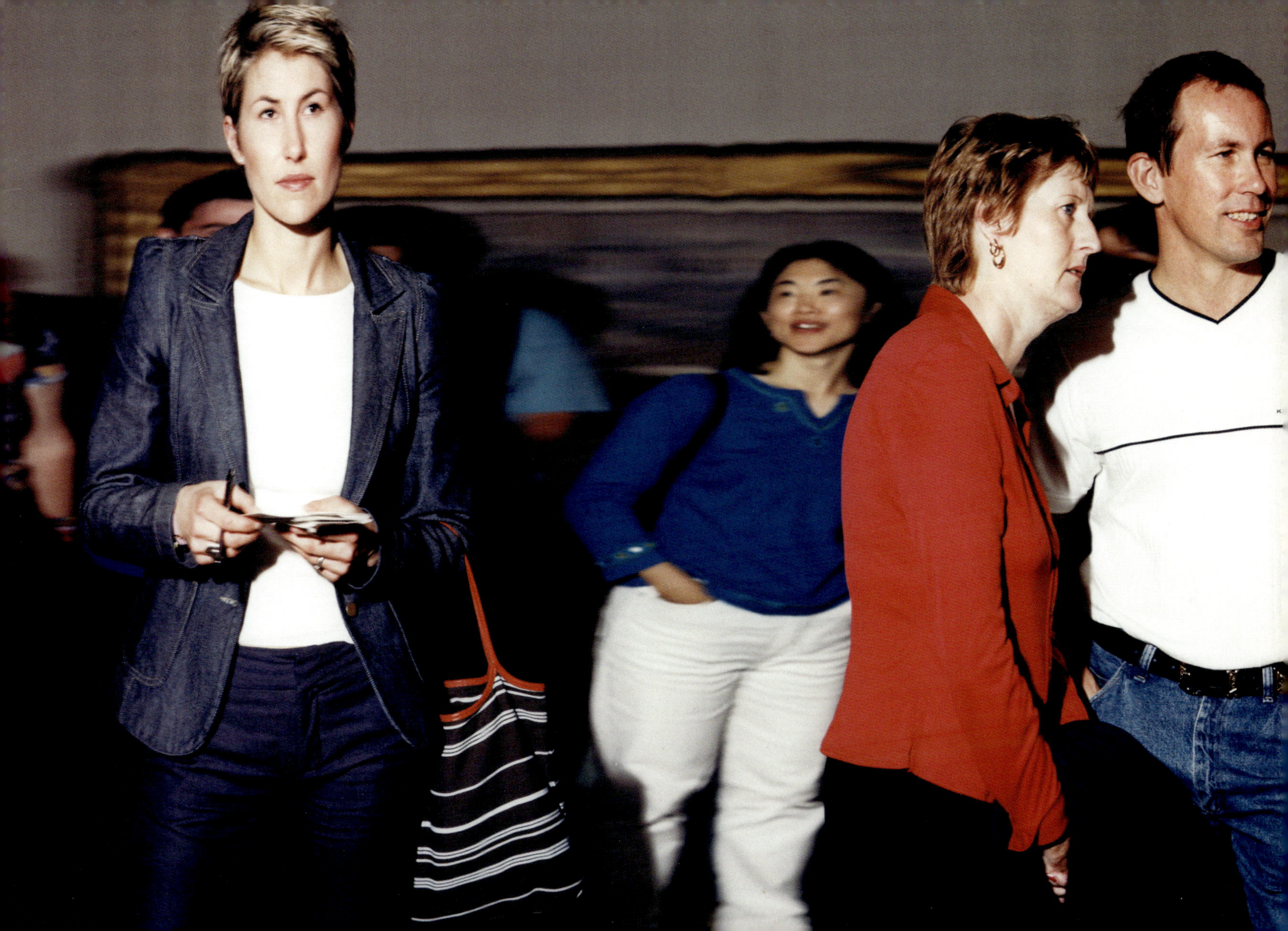

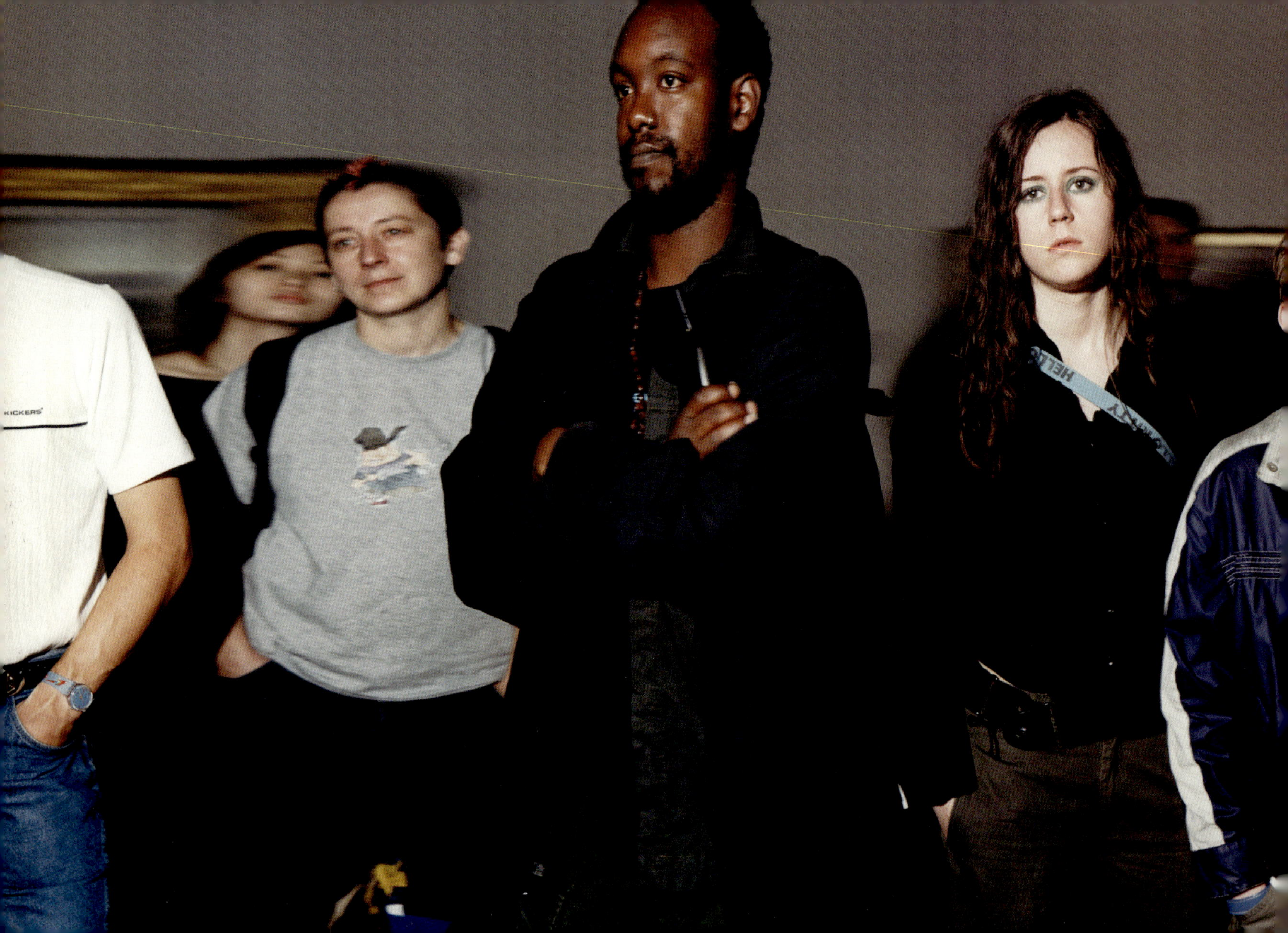
KICKERS

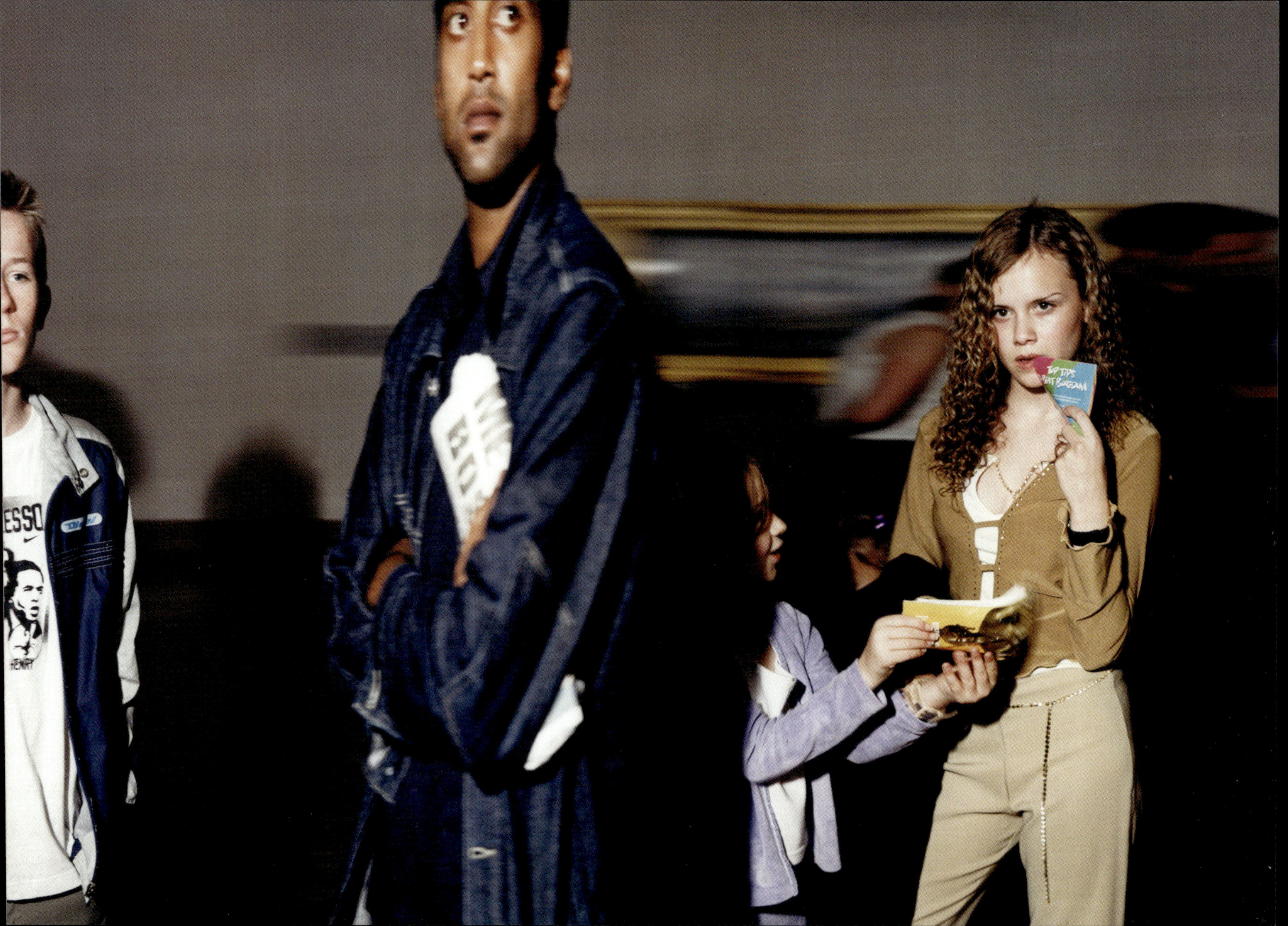
TOP TIPS
HENRY

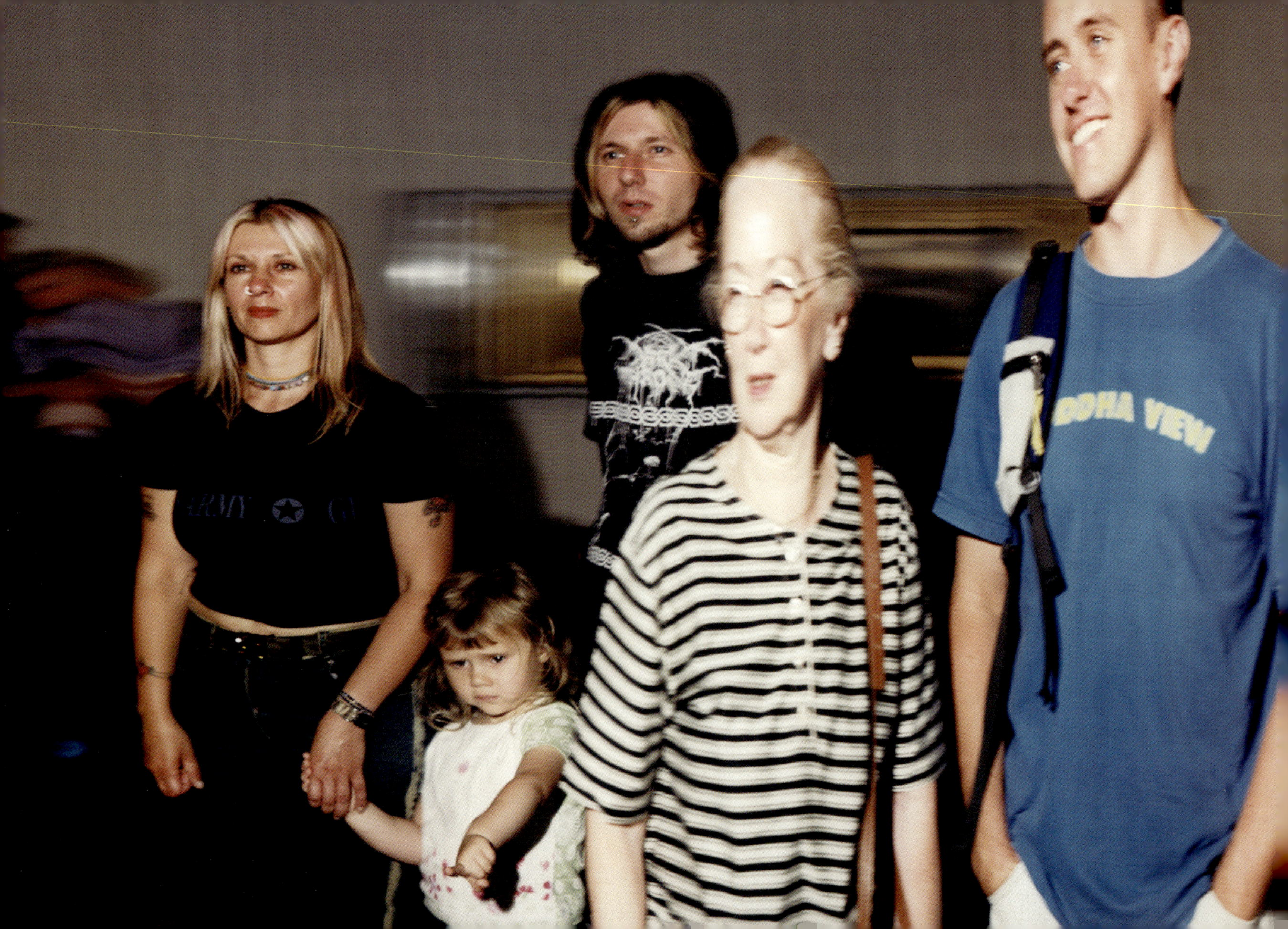

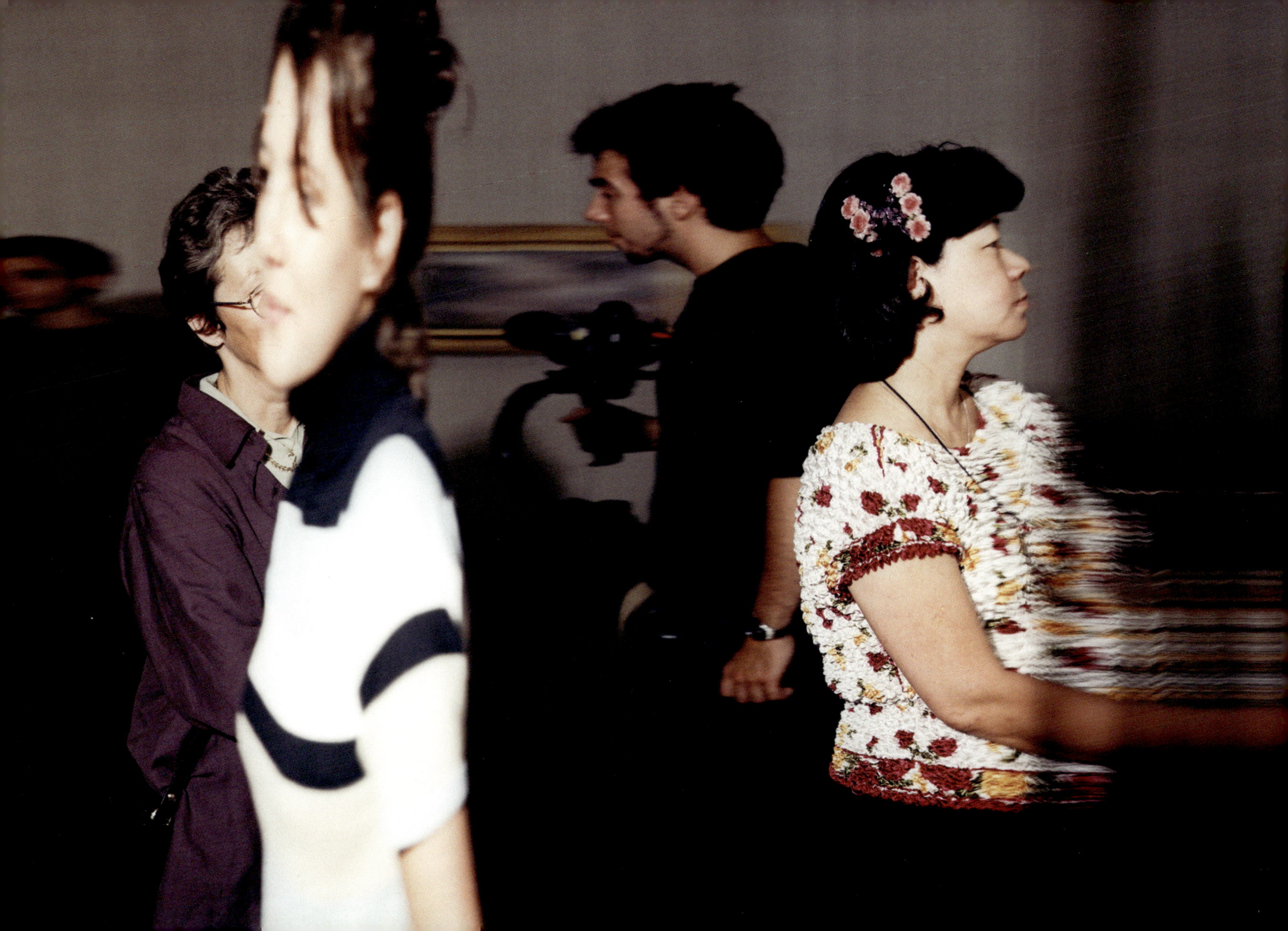

EADWEARD**MUYBRIDGE**

Having established himself as one of the outstanding photographers of the American West, in 1872 Eadweard Muybridge accepted a challenge to produce a single image that would reveal if there were moments in the trot or gallop when a horse was entirely free of the ground. Muybridge aligned twelve cameras along an outdoor track opposite a lined screen, the camera's shutters being tripped in rapid succession by a wire stretched across the horse's path. Muybridge's aim was two-fold: firstly to reduce exposure times in order to get close to the so-called 'instantaneous' image; and secondly, to multiply a sequence of instantaneous snapshots so as to record a passage of time and movement. Using these methods Muybridge succeeded in producing the first serial photographs of each phase of the horse in motion in 1878. Muybridge increased his cameras to 20 and then 24

Plate 627. Animals and Movements. Horses; Gallop; saddle; bay horse. *(Daisy)*. 1887
Phases of Movement Illustrated. Laterals, 20; Quantity of Movement, 1; Time, 23 Thousands of a Second

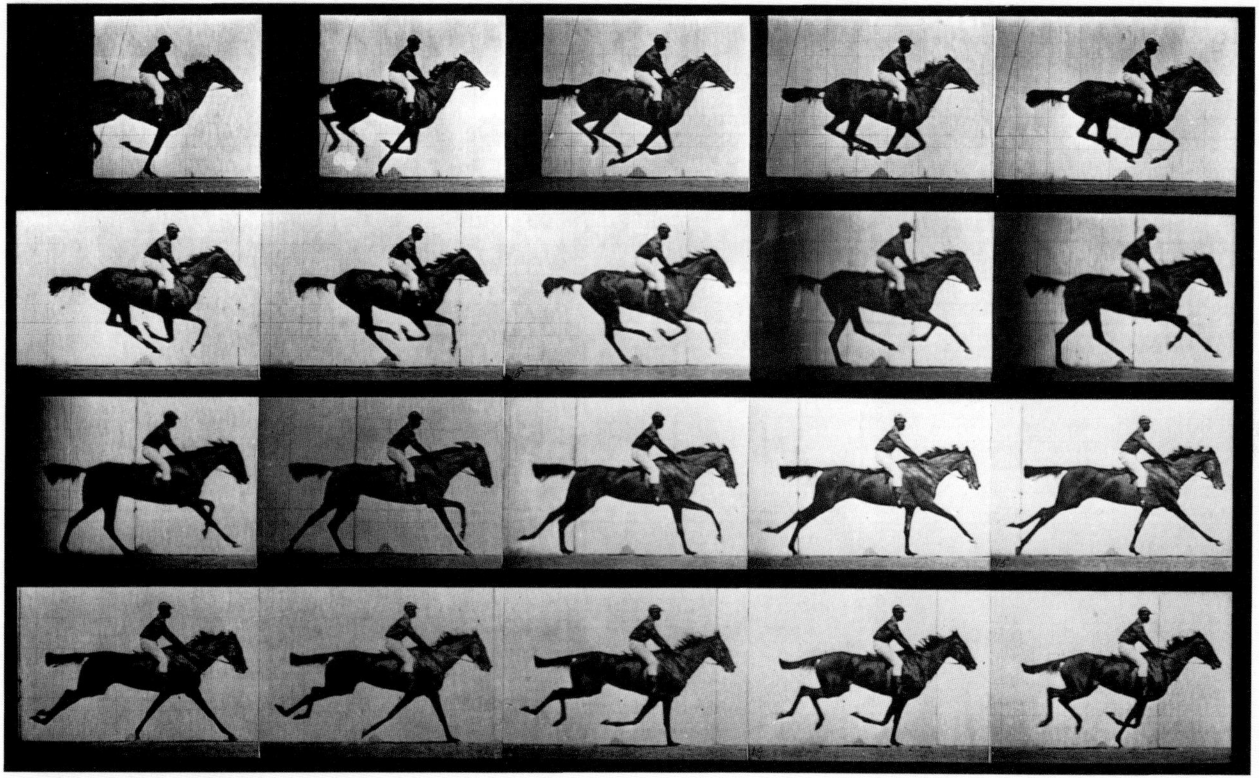

so as to extend the number of individual images within a sequence, thus breaking down the intervals of time and motion represented into ever smaller fragments. Over the next six years he developed more complex multiple camera systems, reduced exposure times to 1/1000th of a second, and created a special studio marked with a horizontal and vertical grid in which to work. He expanded the cast of subjects to include various wild and domesticated animals, and extended the

range of movements - from typical movements: walking, running, sitting etc to social movements: washing, ironing, gardening etc - he asked his subjects to perform. By the mid 1880s he was photographing men, women and children playing out chosen stories for the scrutiny of three batteries of twelve cameras: one parallel to the subject ("laterals"), the other two at 60 or 90 degrees ("foreshortenings"), each armed with a new electro-magnetic device to

Plate 45. Movements. Walking, two models meeting, and partly turning; Models, 4 *(unmarried aged seventeen to twenty-four)*, 16 *(married)*; Costume, Draped. Fully clothed. 1887
Phases of Movement Illustrated. Laterals, 24; Quantity of Movement, 2; Time, 78 Thousands of a Second

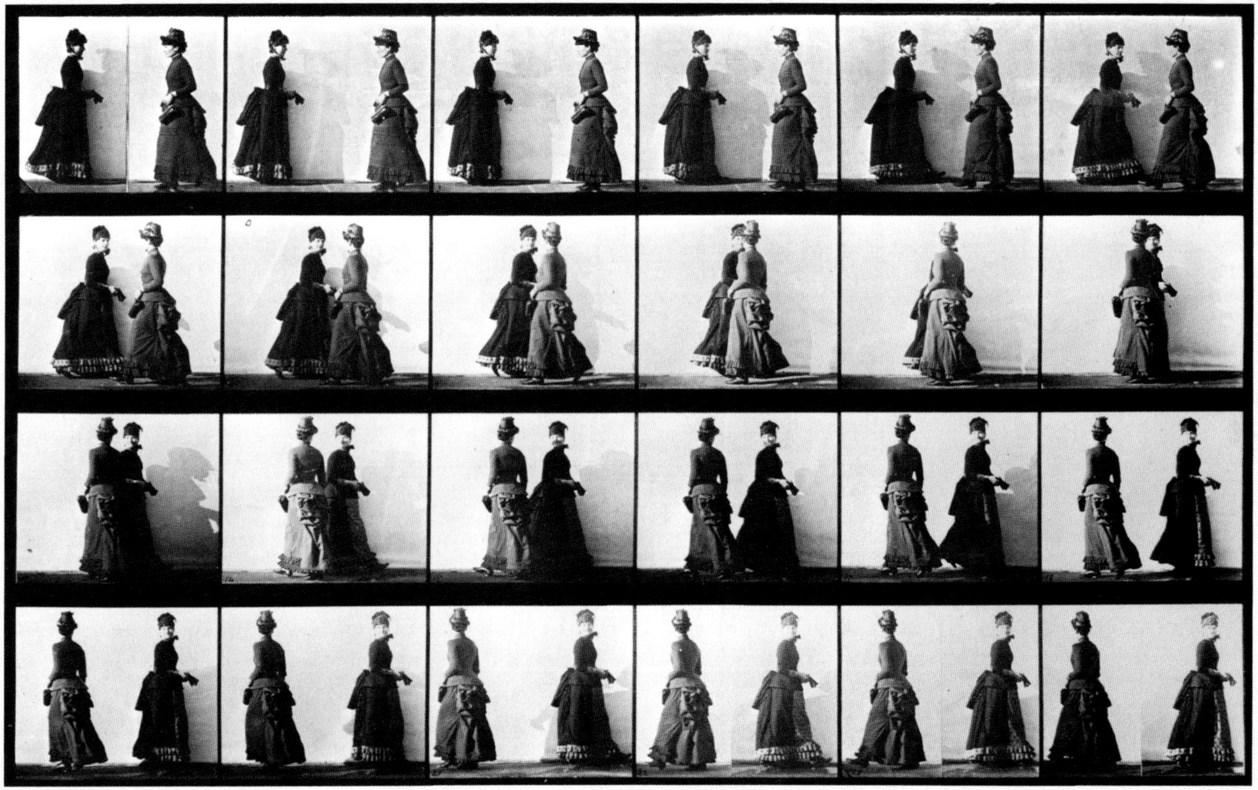

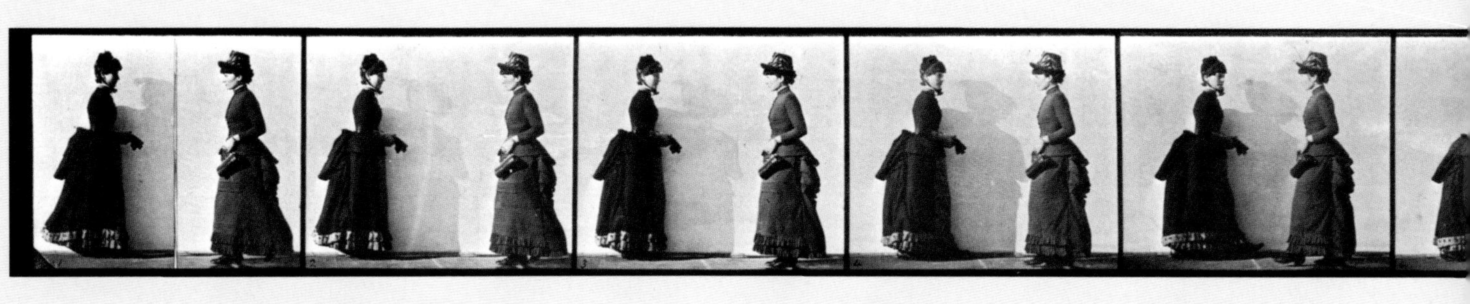

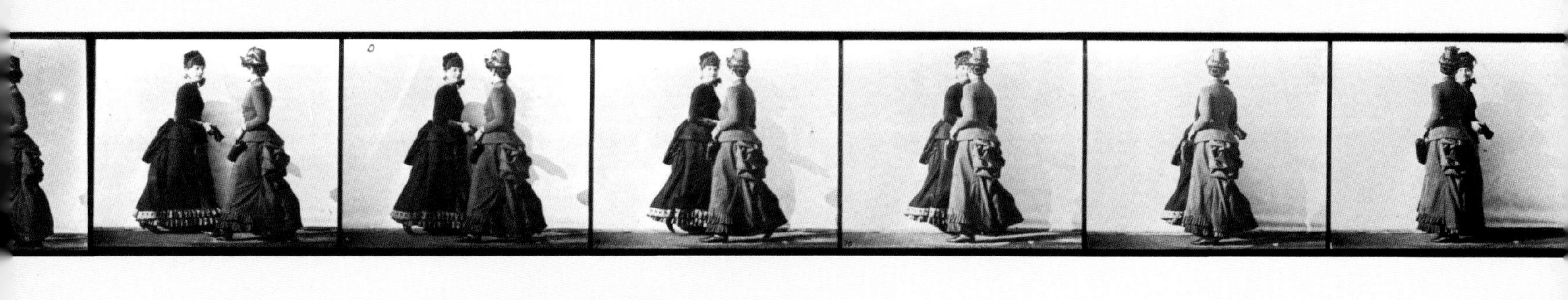

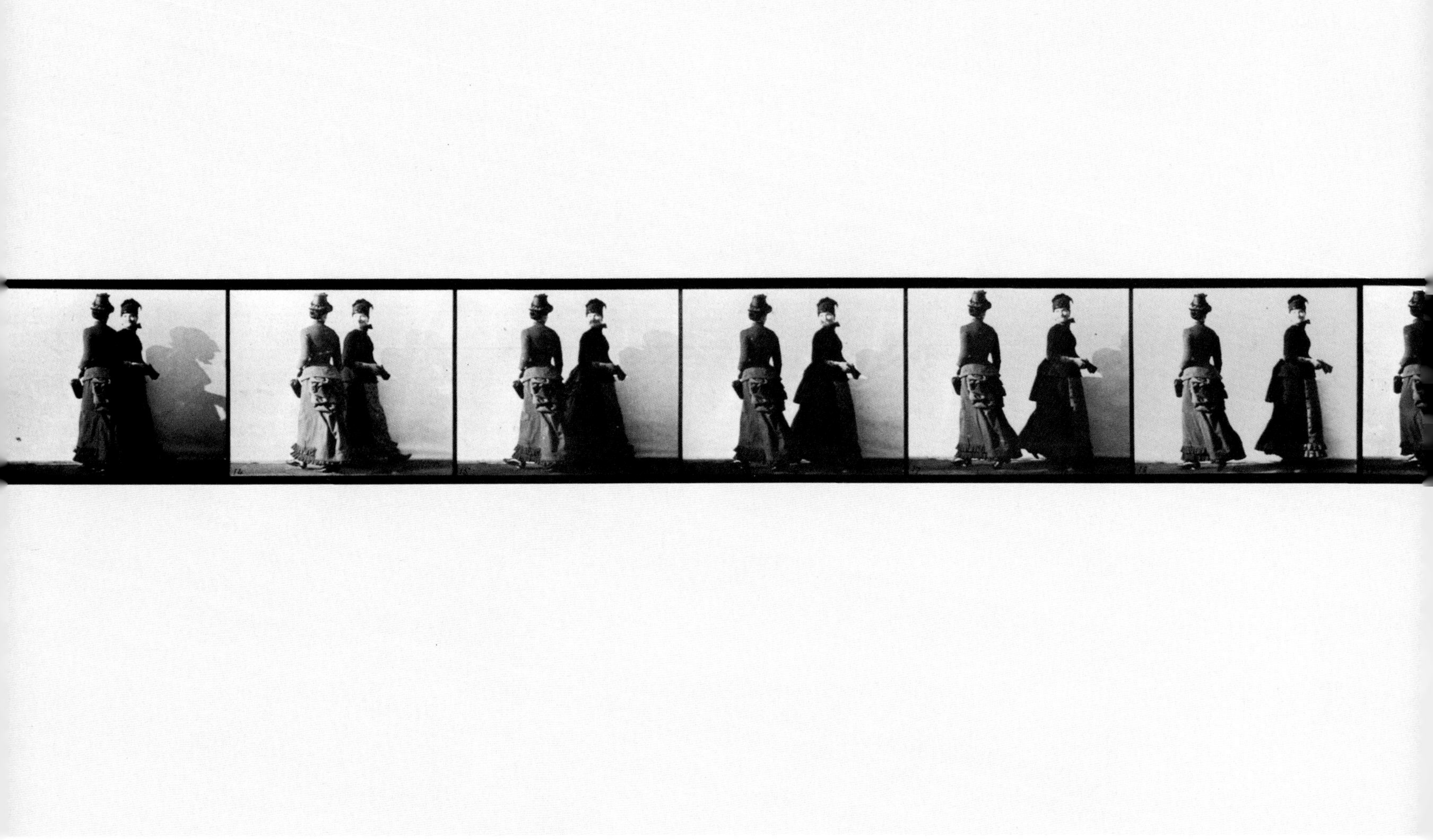

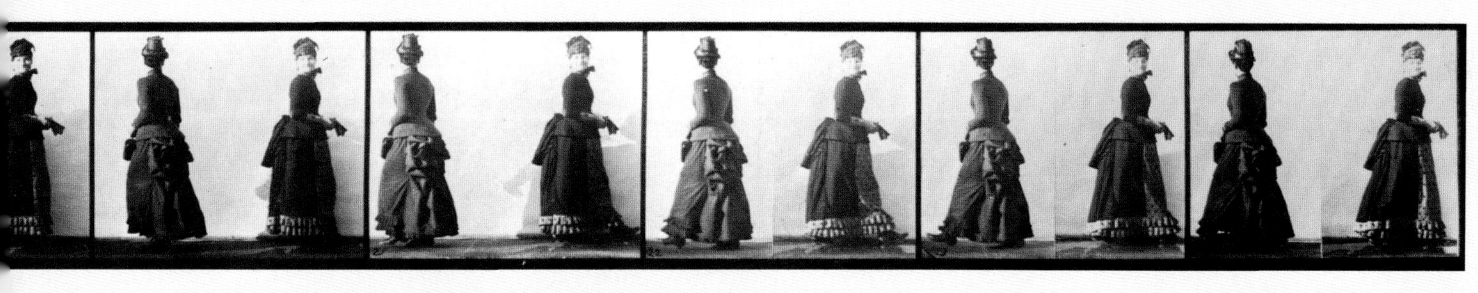

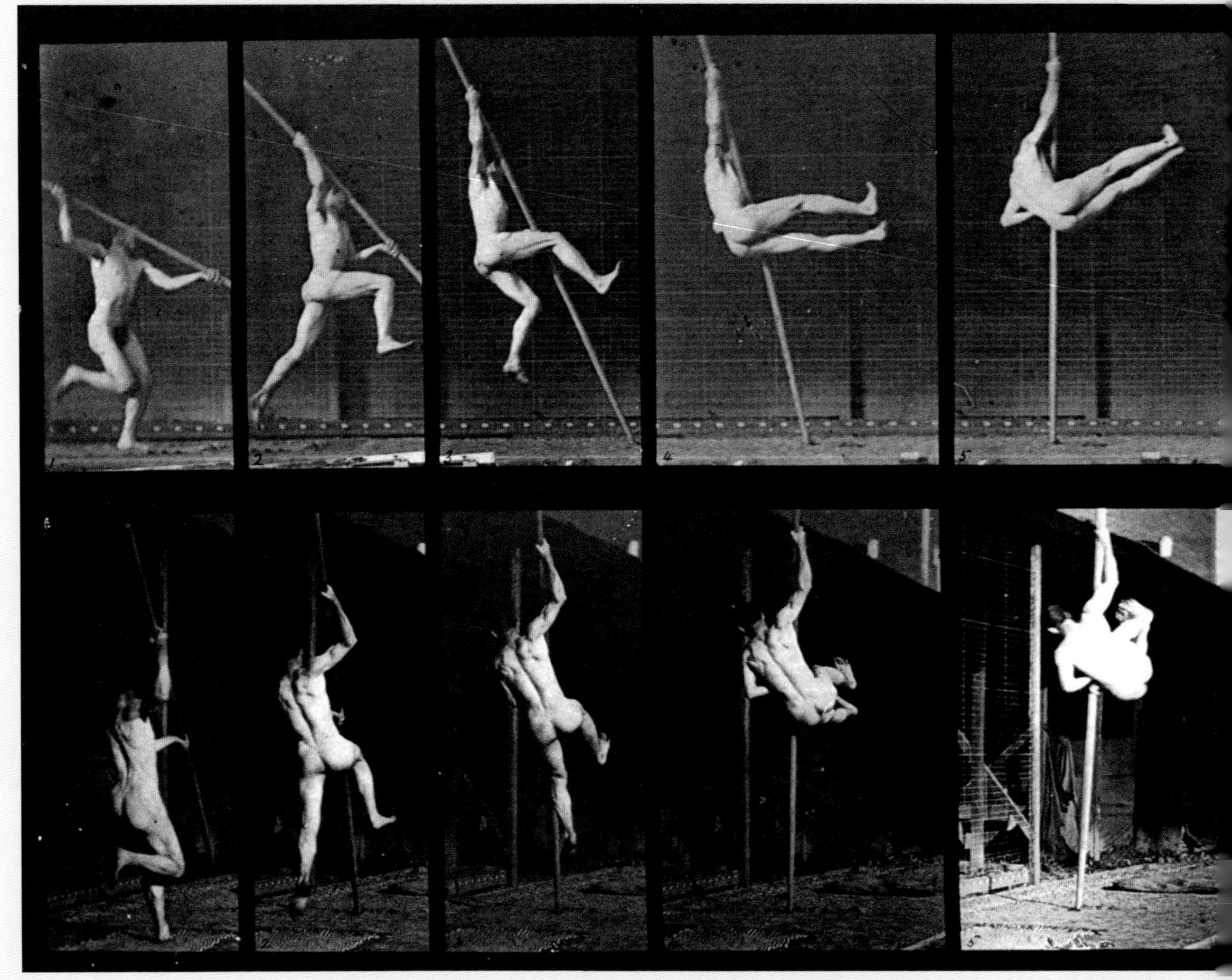

Plate 164. Movements. Jumping; pole vaulting; Model, 46 *(student or graduate of The University of Pennsylvania - aged between eighteen to twenty-four)*; Costume, Nude. 1887
Phases of Movement Illustrated. Laterals, 11; Foreshortenings. Rear 60°, 11; Quantity of Movement, 1

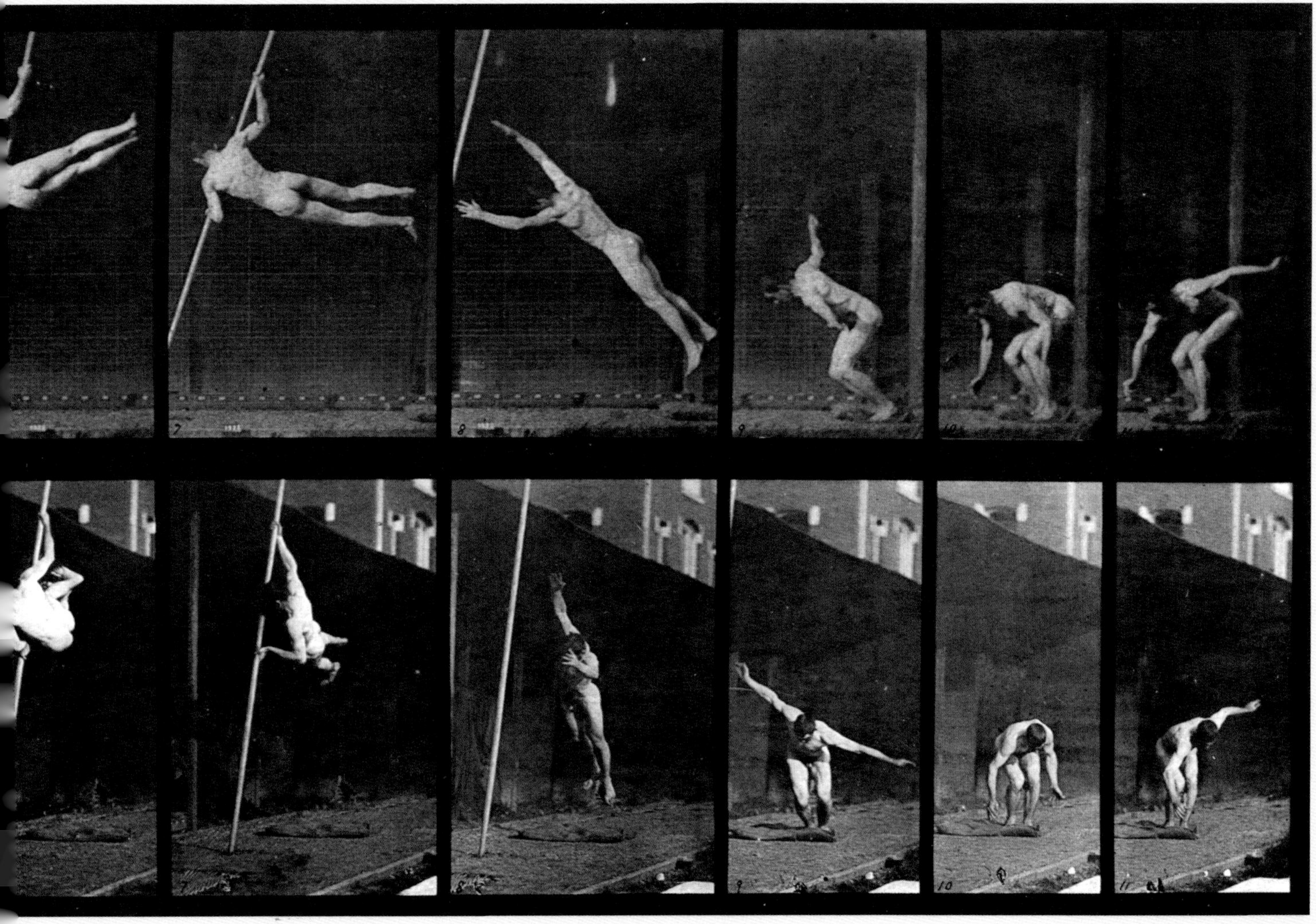

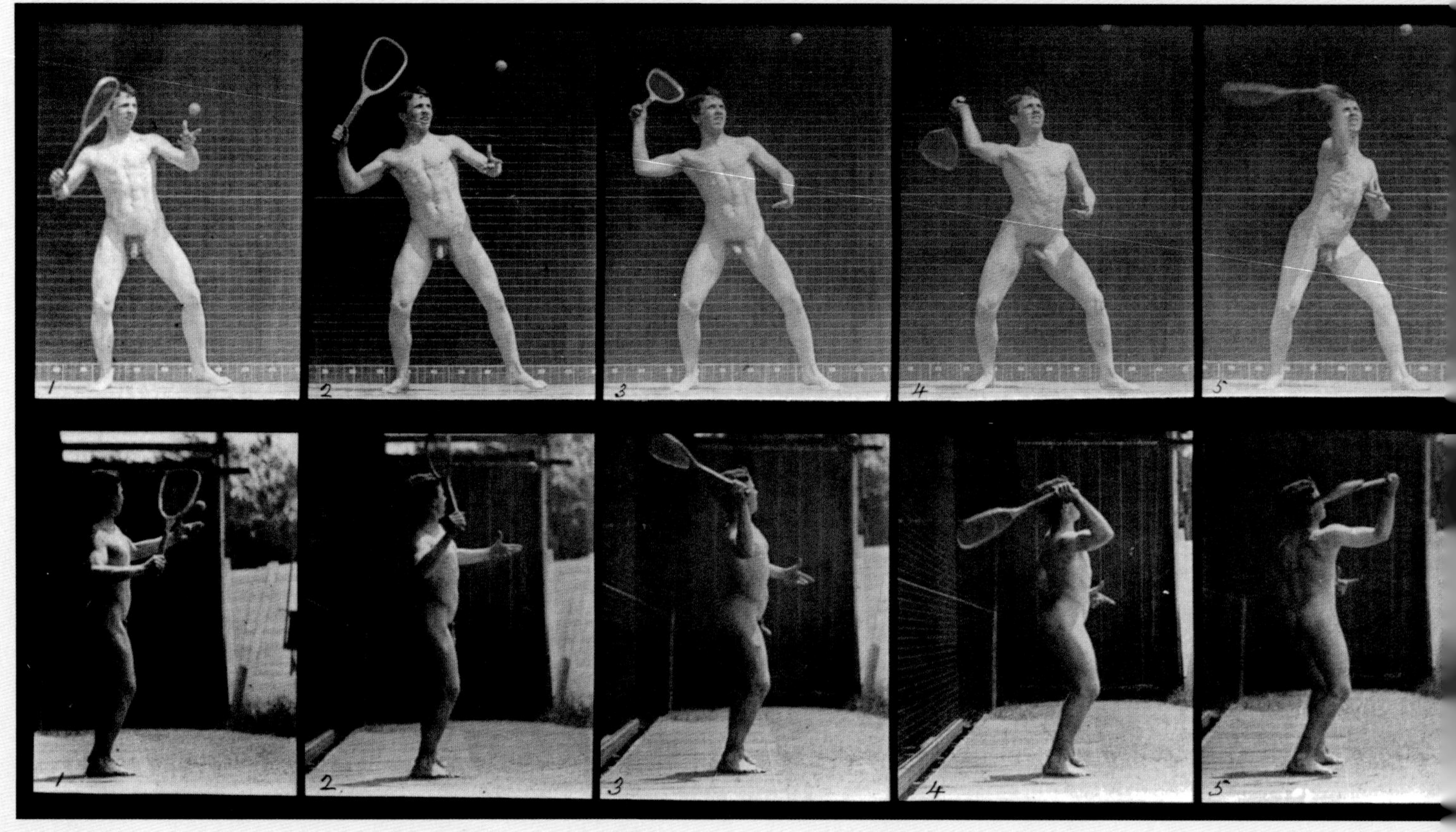

Plate 294. Movements. Lawn tennis; serving; Model, 25 *(student or graduate of The University of Pennsylvania - aged between eighteen to twenty-four)*; Costume, Nude. 1887
Phases of Movement Illustrated. Laterals, 10; Foreshortenings. Rear 90°, 10; Quantity of Movement, 1; Time, 101 Thousands of a Second

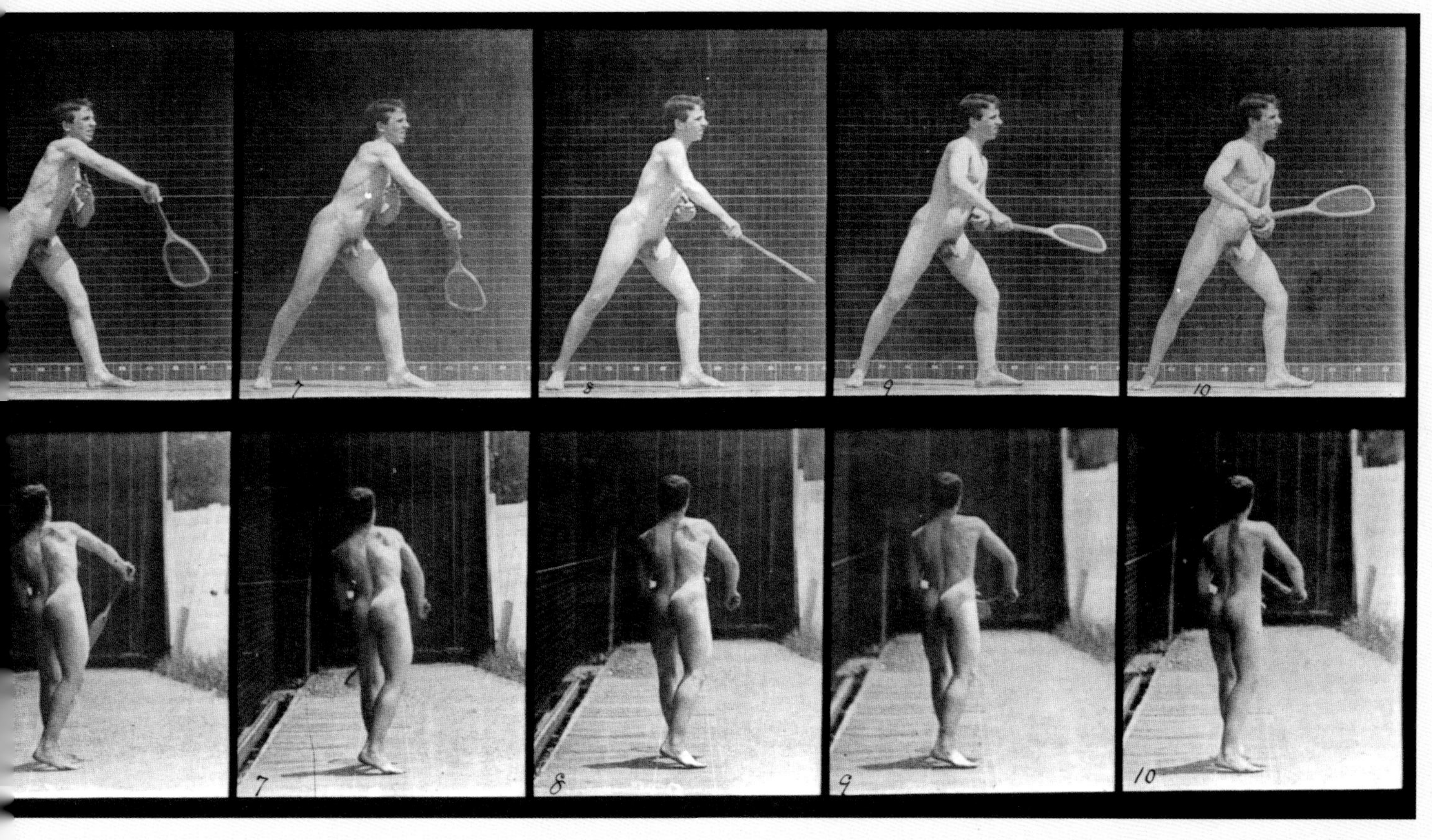

Reference Notes; A double interval of time, respectively, between phases 5 and 6; 7 and 8

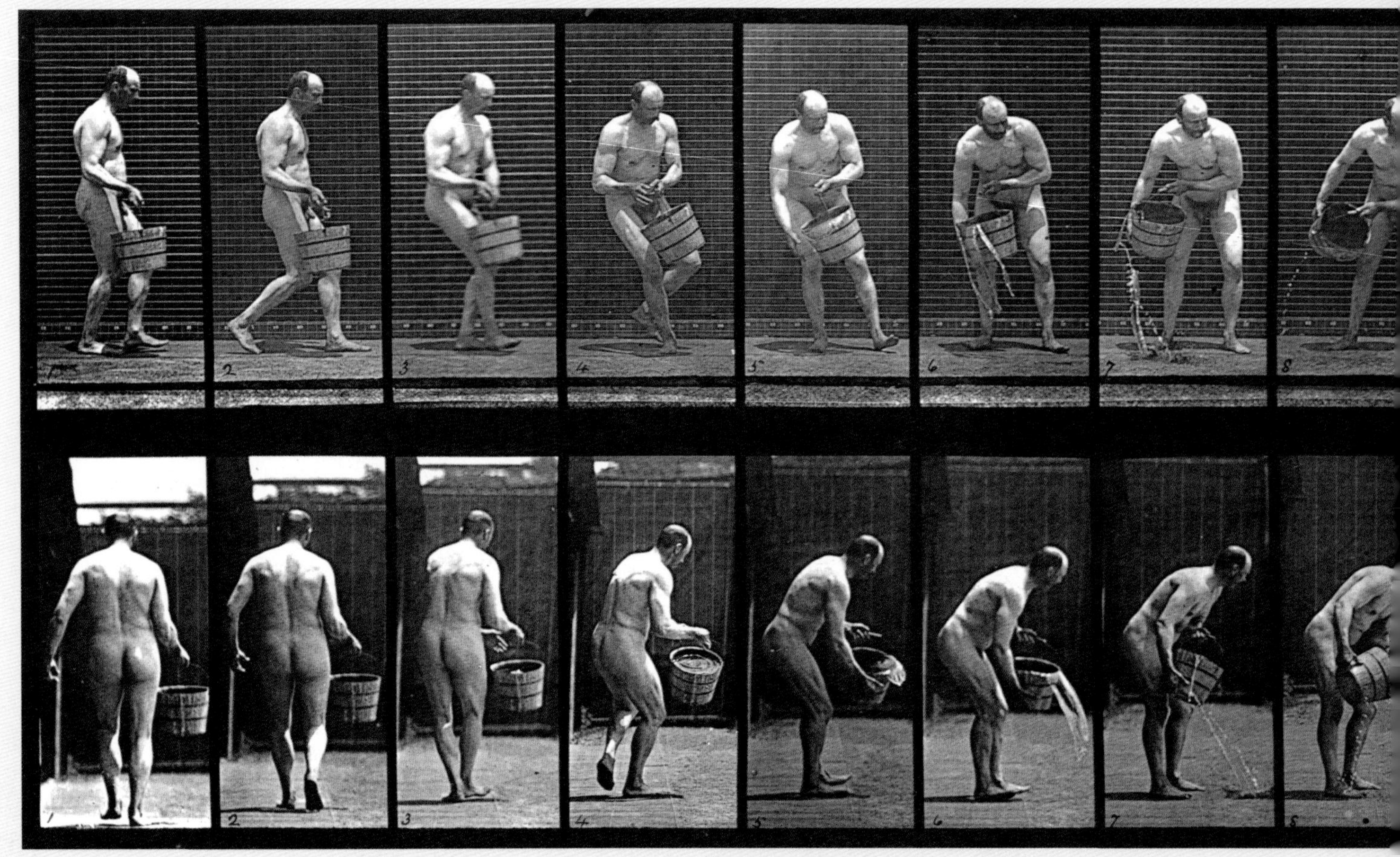

Plate 399. Movements. Emptying bucket of water; Model, 39 *(student or graduate of The University of Pennsylvania - aged between eighteen to twenty-four)*; Costume, Nude. 1887
Phases of Movement Illustrated. Laterals, 12; Foreshortenings. Rear 90°, 12; Quantity of Movement, 1; Time, 209 Thousands of a Second

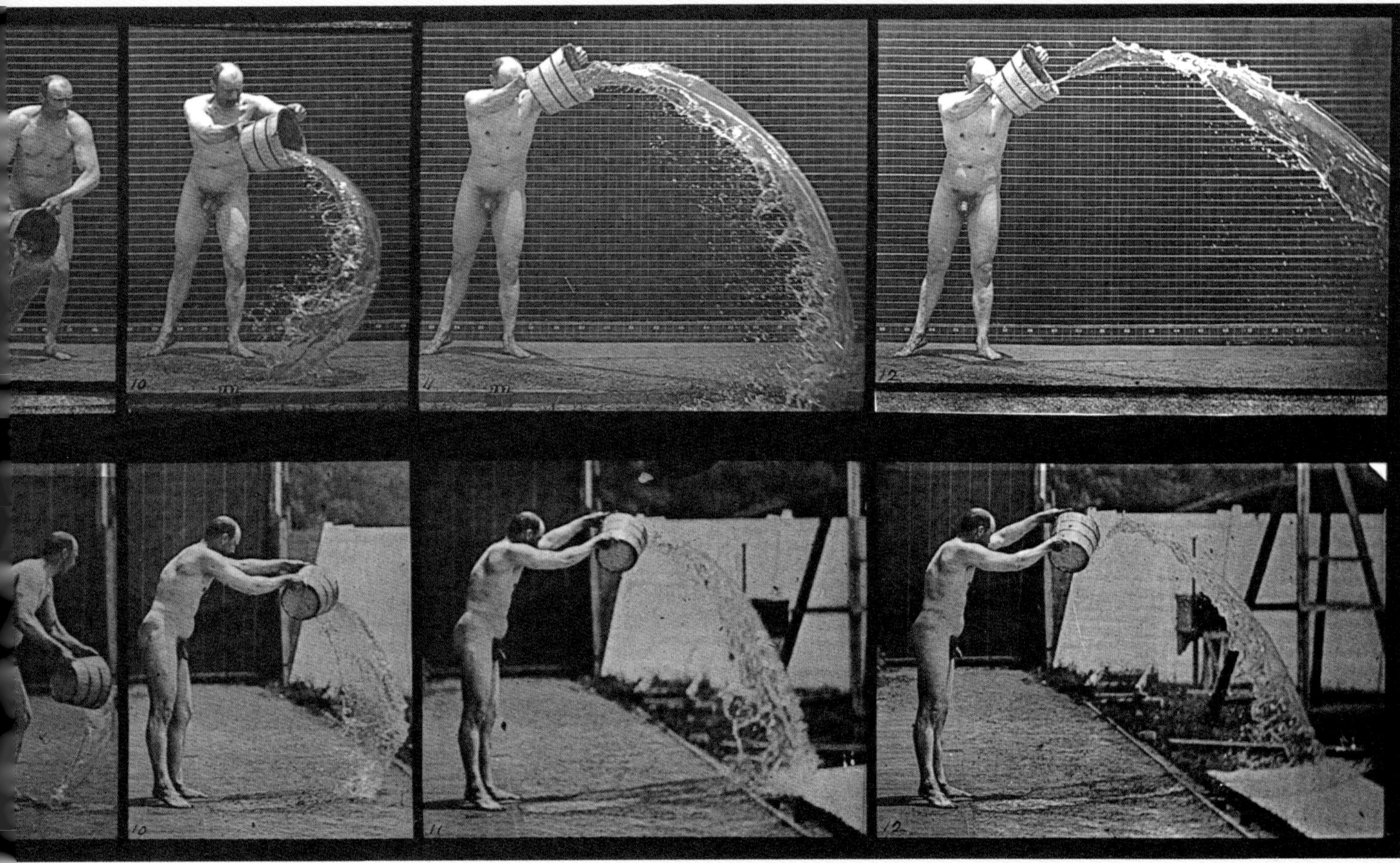
10
11
12
10
11
12

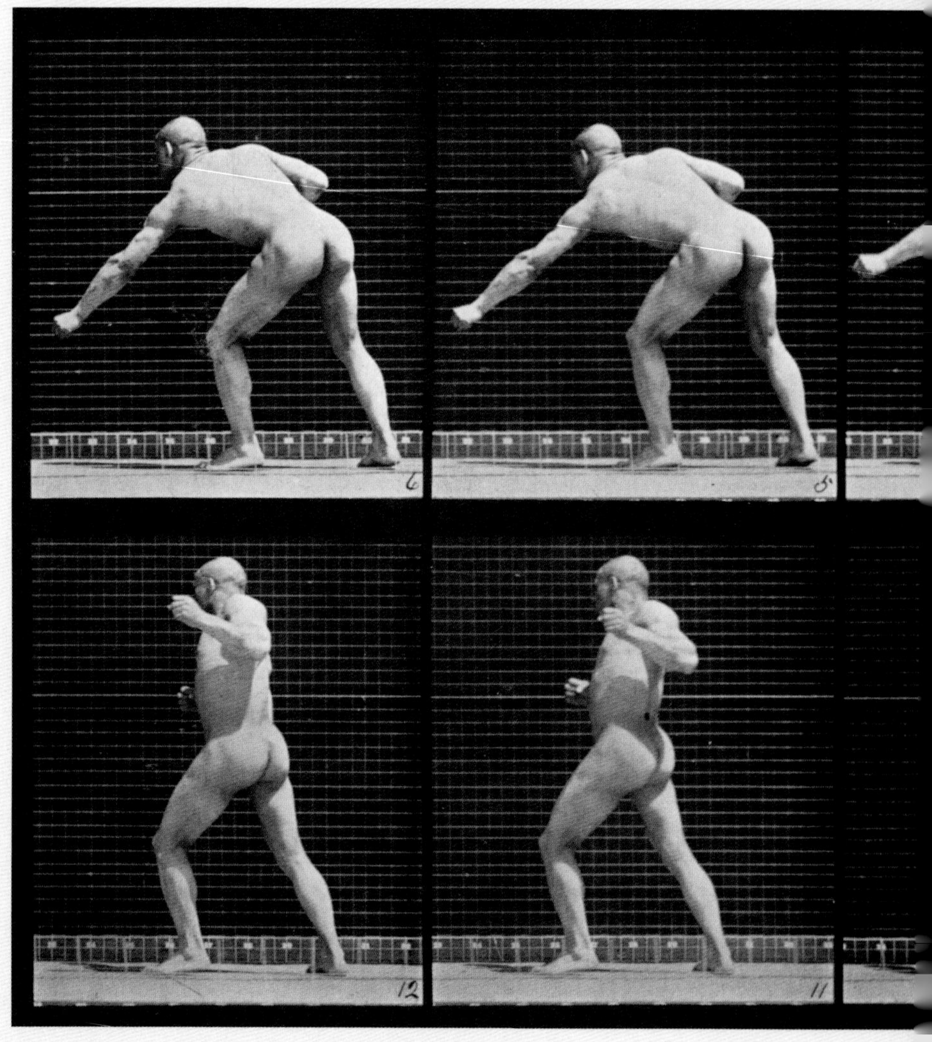

Plate 343. Movements. Striking a blow (left hand); Model, 22 *(a mulatto and professional pugilist)*; Costume, Nude. 1887
Phases of Movement Illustrated. Laterals, 12; Quantity of Movement, 1; Time, 124 Thousands of a Second

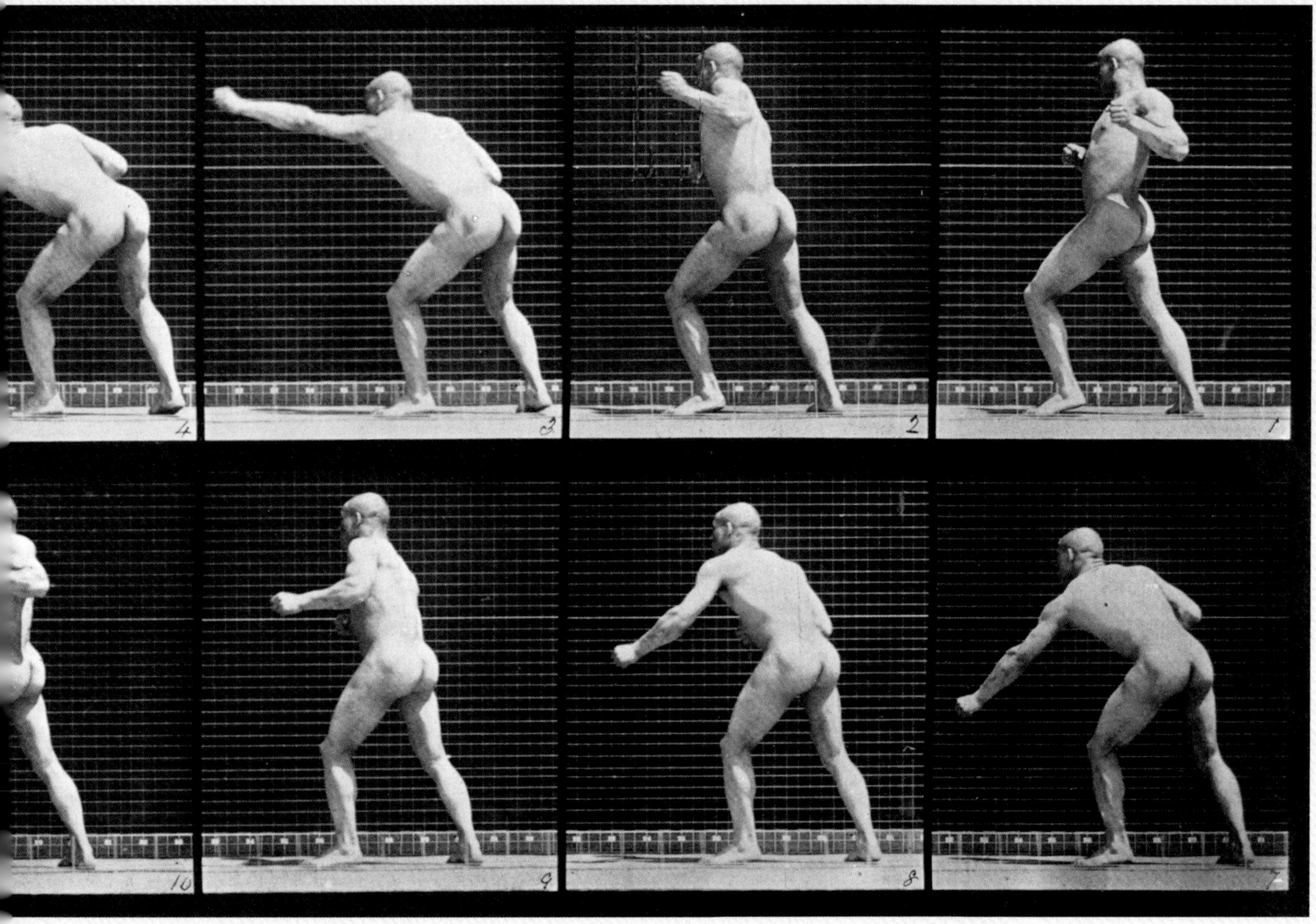

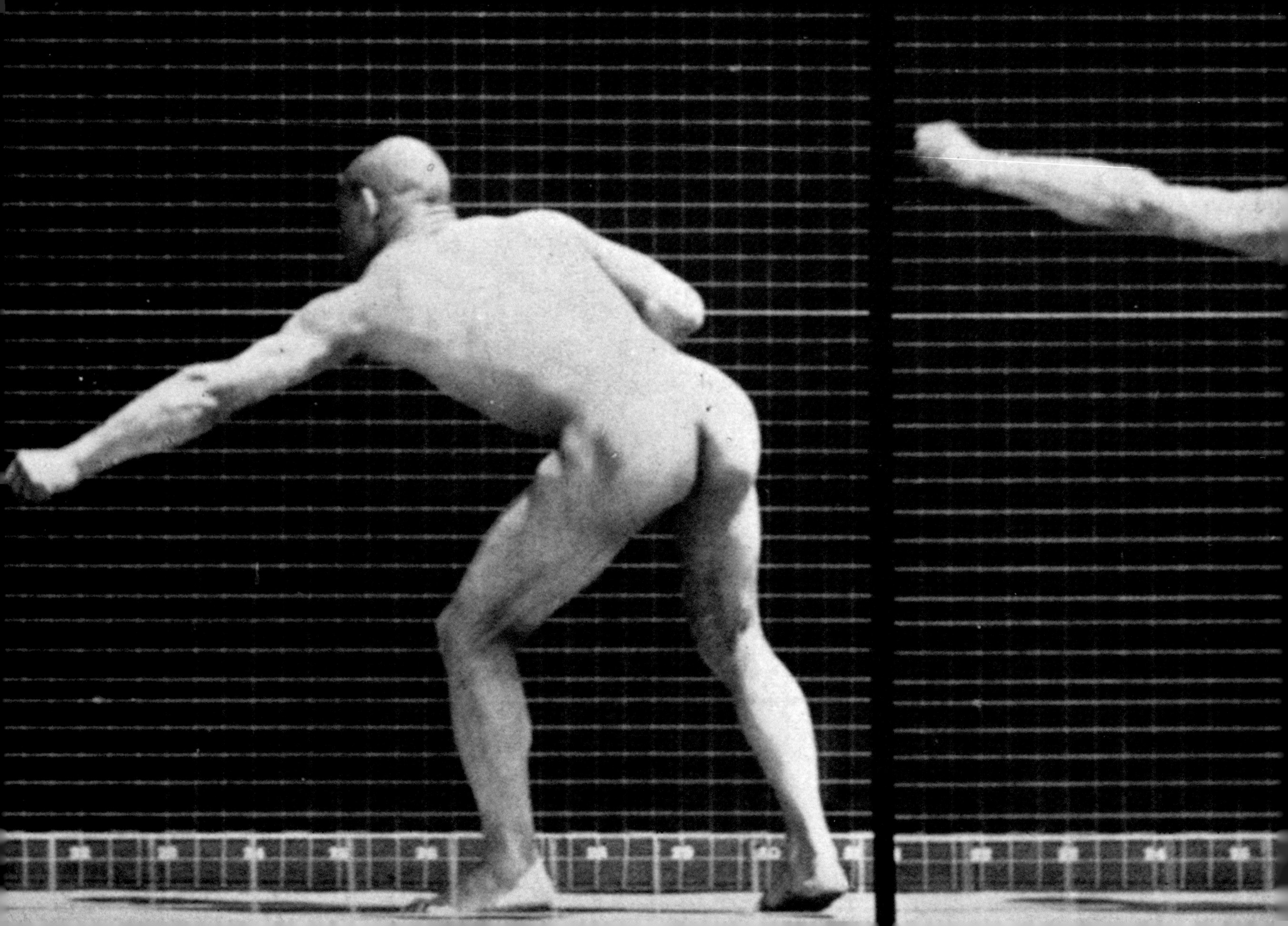

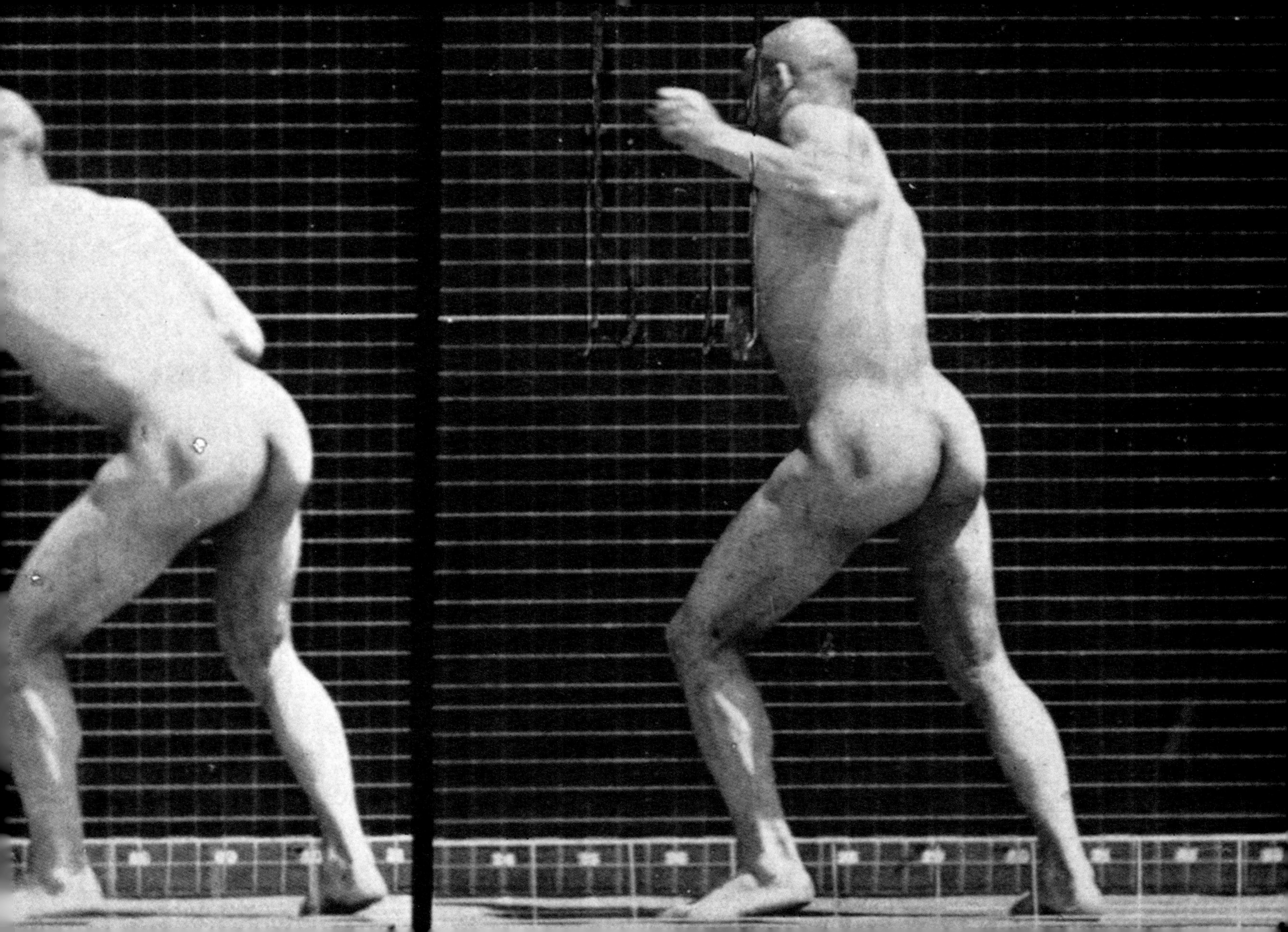

operate the shutters. The result of this work, Animal Locomotion: An Electro-Photographic Investigation of Consecutive Phases of Animal Movements - eleven volumes containing a total of 781 plates assembled from 19,347 single images - was offered for publication by subscription in 1887.

Muybridge's daily notebooks reveal that with few exceptions he made twelve lateral and twenty four foreshortenings of each subject. However, in about only half of the

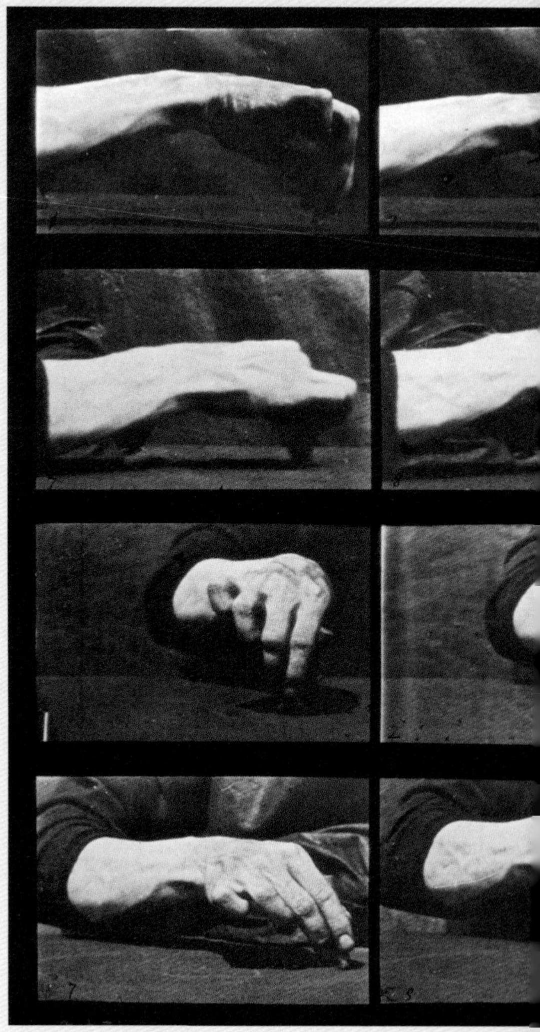

Plate 532. Movements. Movement of the hand; drawing a circle; Model, 51 *(a well-known instructor in art)*. 1887
Phases of Movement Illustrated. Laterals, 12; Foreshortenings. Front 90°, 12; Quantity of Movement, 1; Time, 124 Thousands of a Second

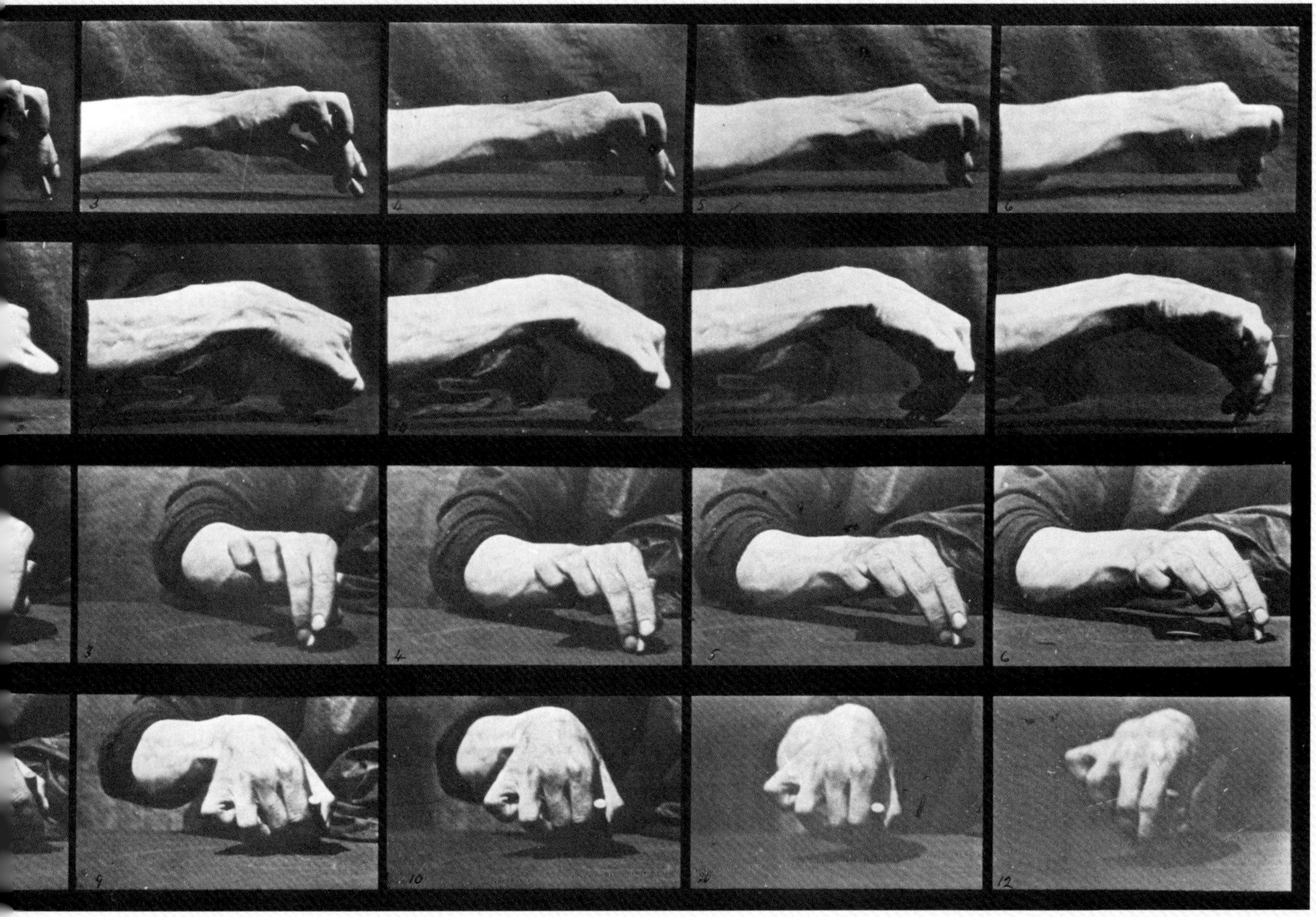

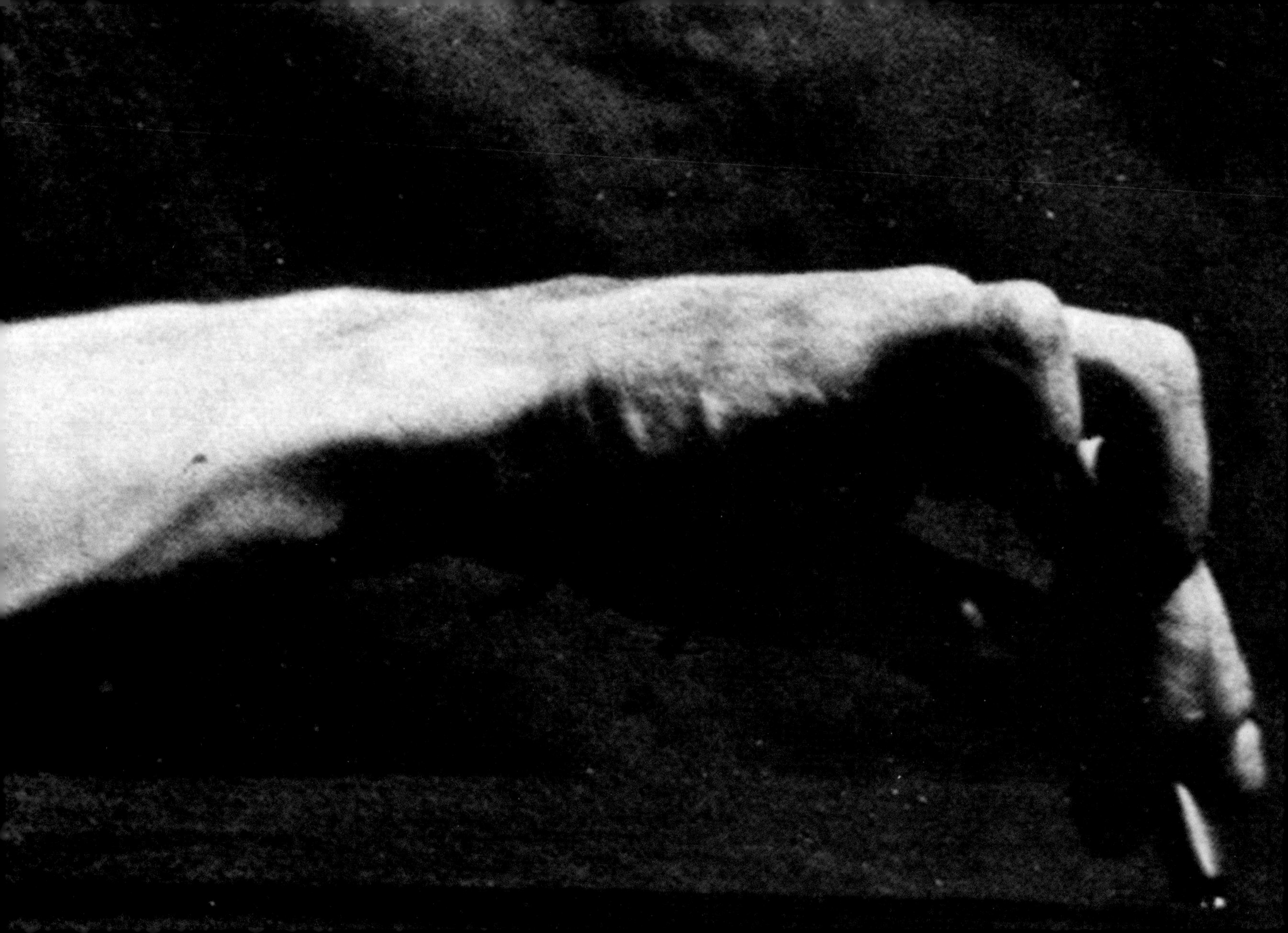

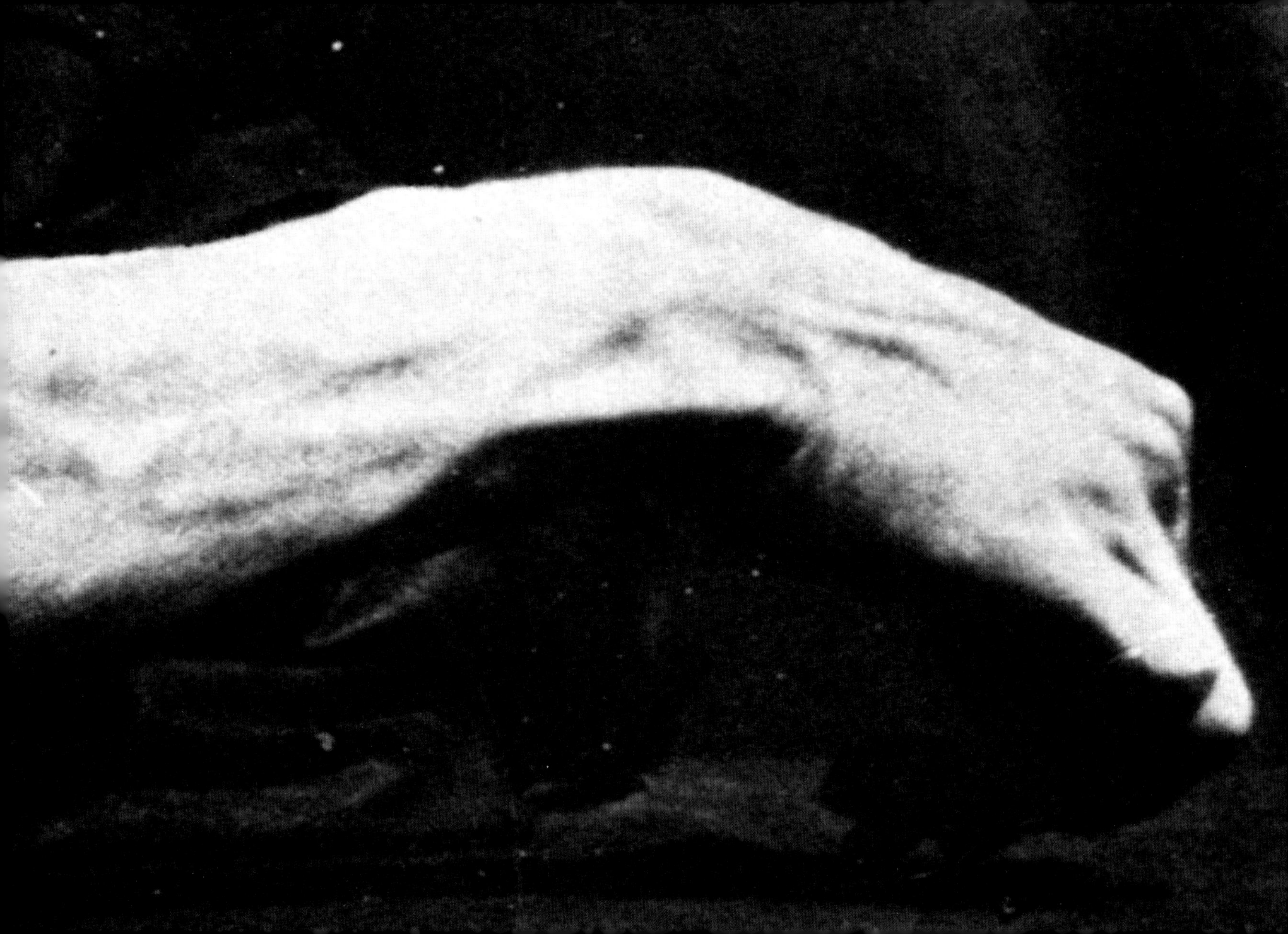

published prints did all thirty six images appear intact. The others, whilst giving the appearance of sequential images, are in fact assemblages whose careful editing and arrangement dictates our perception of the individual image, the finished print and the time and motion represented within them. Further to this, the notation concerning the differing intervals of time

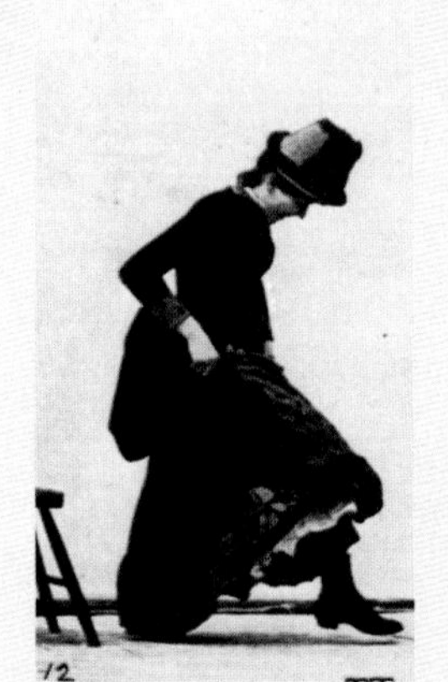

between each image is also of interest. The majority show a direct relationship with the speed of the movement photographed. However, some plates reveal the recording of simultaneous images across the batteries of cameras. It appears that the recording of complete movement in all its phases and the exact time elapsed was less important to Muybridge than a pictorially acceptable final print.

Pete James

Plate 365. Movements. Head-spring, a flying pigeon interfering; Model, 42 *(public acrobat)*; Costume, Pelvis Cloth. A strip of cloth surrounds the lower part of the abdomen. 1887
Phases of Movement Illustrated. Laterals, 12; Foreshortenings. Front 90°, 12; Quantity of Movement, 1; Time, 85 Thousands of a Second

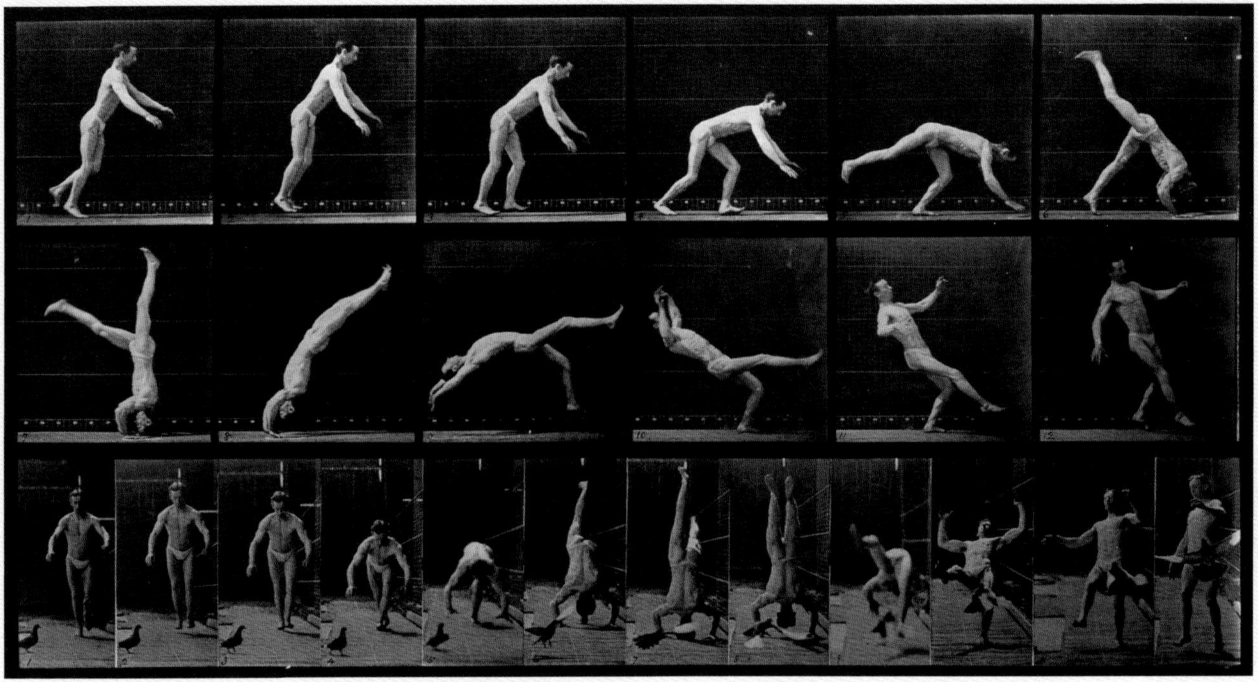

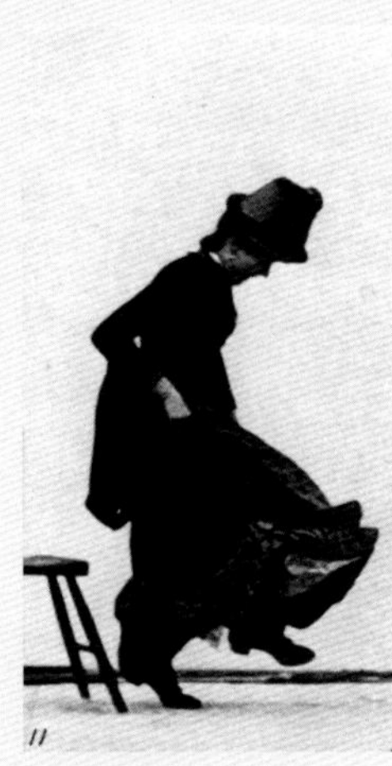

Plate 502. Movements. Miscellaneous,- stooping, kneeling, etc; Model, 7 *(unmarried, aged from seventeen to twenty-four)*; Costume, Transparent Drapery. 1887
Phases of Movement Illustrated. Laterals, 9; Foreshortenings. Front 60°, 9, Rear 60°, 9

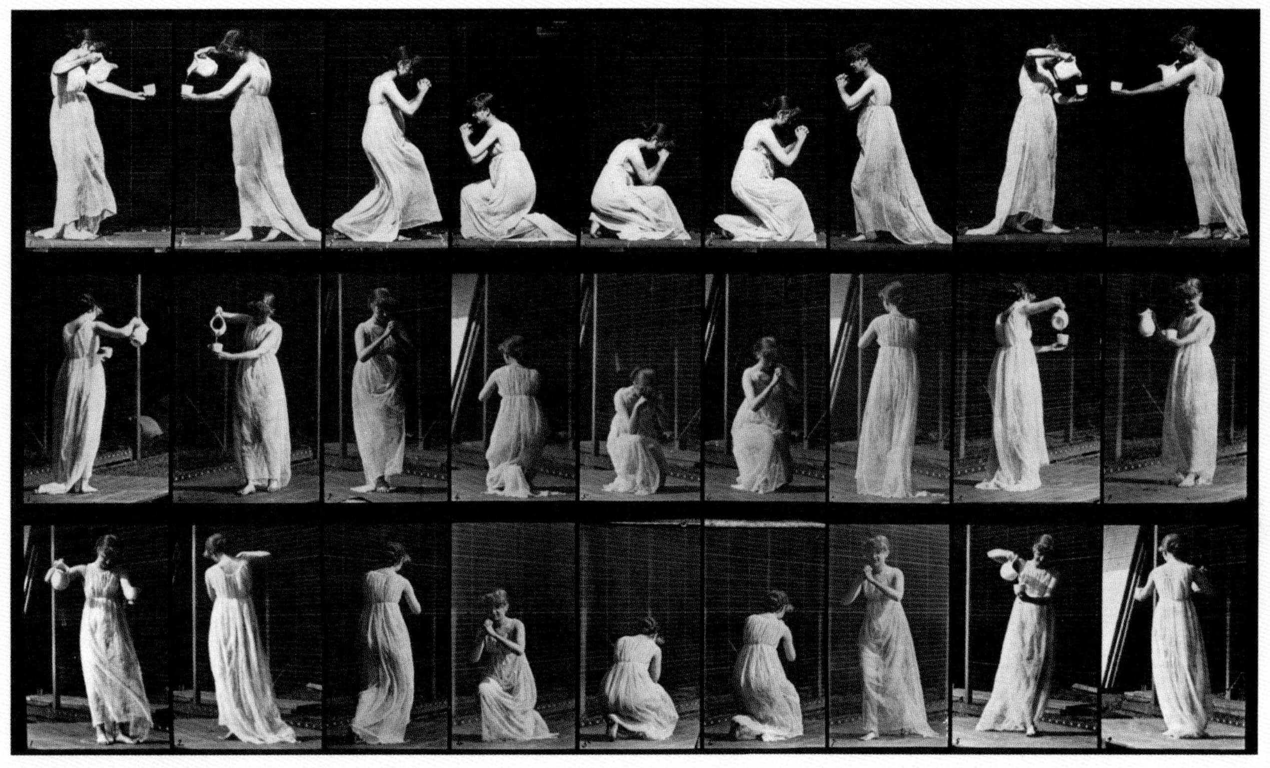

The model is attired in a flowing garment of diaphanous texture, which permits the action of the limbs to be seen, and the conformation of the folds of the drapery thereto
Reference Notes; Isolated phases, photographed synchronously from the various points of view

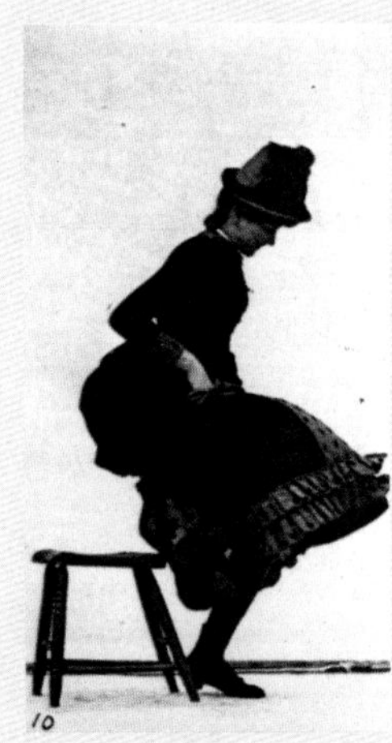

Plate 521. Movements. A, walking; B, ascending step; C, throwing disk; D, using shovel; E, using pick; F, using pick; Model, 95 *(an ex-athlete, aged about sixty)*; Costume, Nude. 1887
Phases of Movement Illustrated. Laterals, 12; Foreshortenings. Front 90°, 6, 60°, 6, Rear 90°, 6, 60°, 6

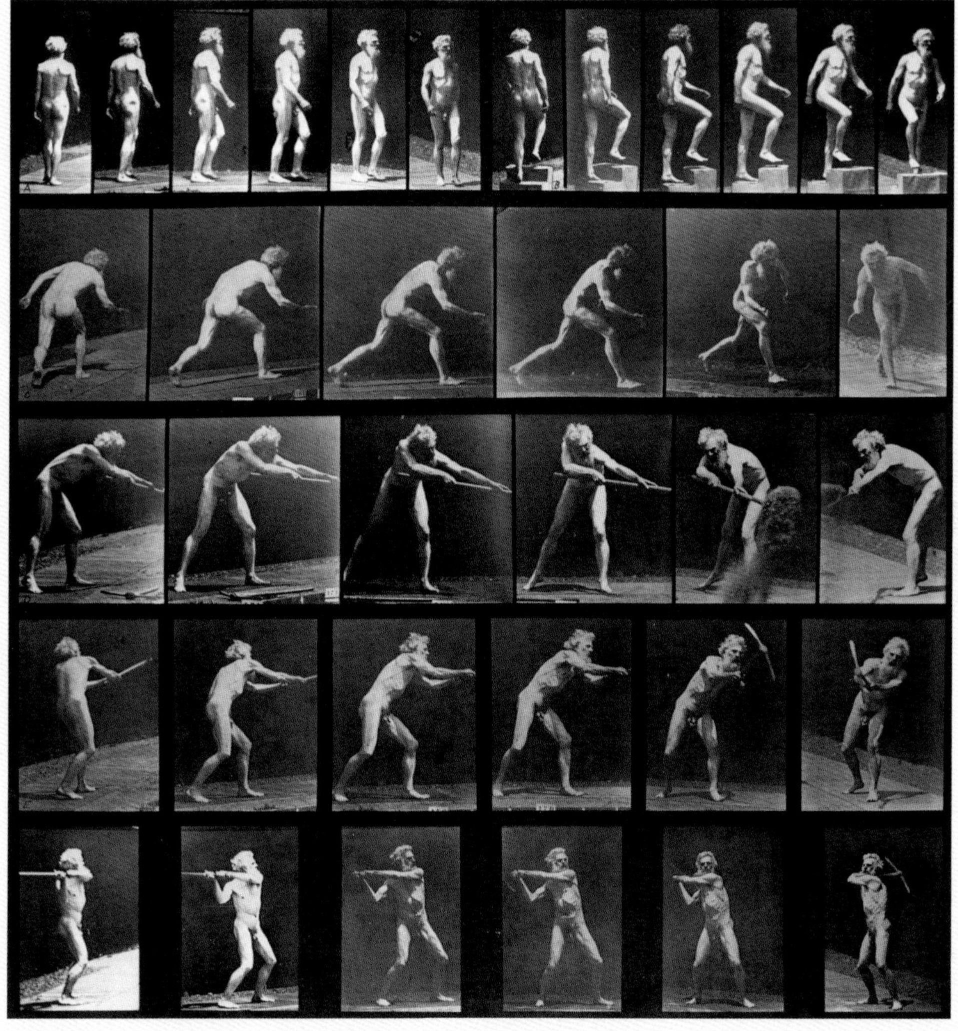

Reference Notes; Isolated phases, photographed synchronously from the various points of view

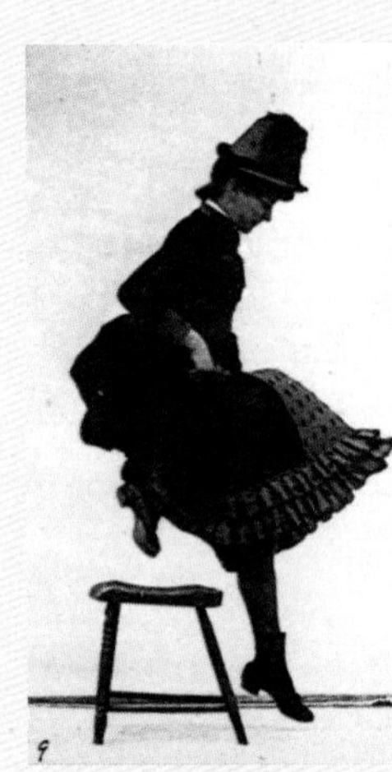

HAROLD**EDGERTON**

Once the problem of fixing the static image from the camera obscura had been resolved, chemists and photographers turned to capturing in a photograph the world in motion. The earliest 'instantaneous' photography was in fact patented by Fox Talbot in 1851, only ten years after he had invented the calotype. This method, known as 'spark photography', whilst elementary in comparison with

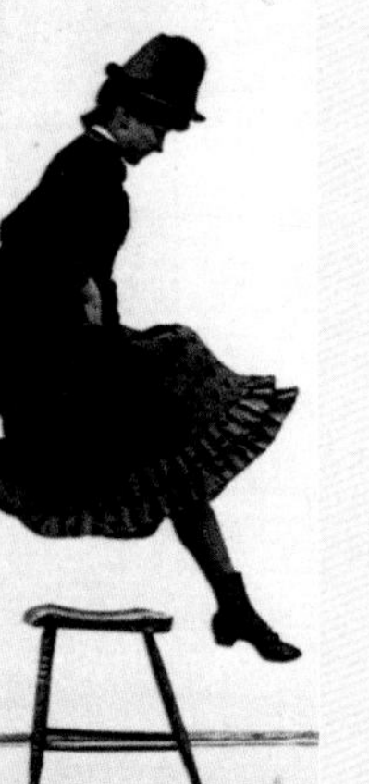

the techniques now being used by Dr. Edgerton, employed the same principles. Since nothing travels faster than light, a spark will stop motion at speeds much higher than those possible using shutters. Talbot used the discharge from a Leyden battery, Dr. Edgerton uses conventional flash tubes. Conventional equipment is used to take high-speed photographs but shutter settings are unimportant because the light can be

Splash of a Milk Drop. 1957. *A drop of milk splashing on a plate creates a crown-shaped form. This is actually the second drop to arrive; the first simply made a disk of milk. The second drop striking the disk pushes up the crown at the edge. The small drop at the top is left over from the stringer of liquid at the intersection*

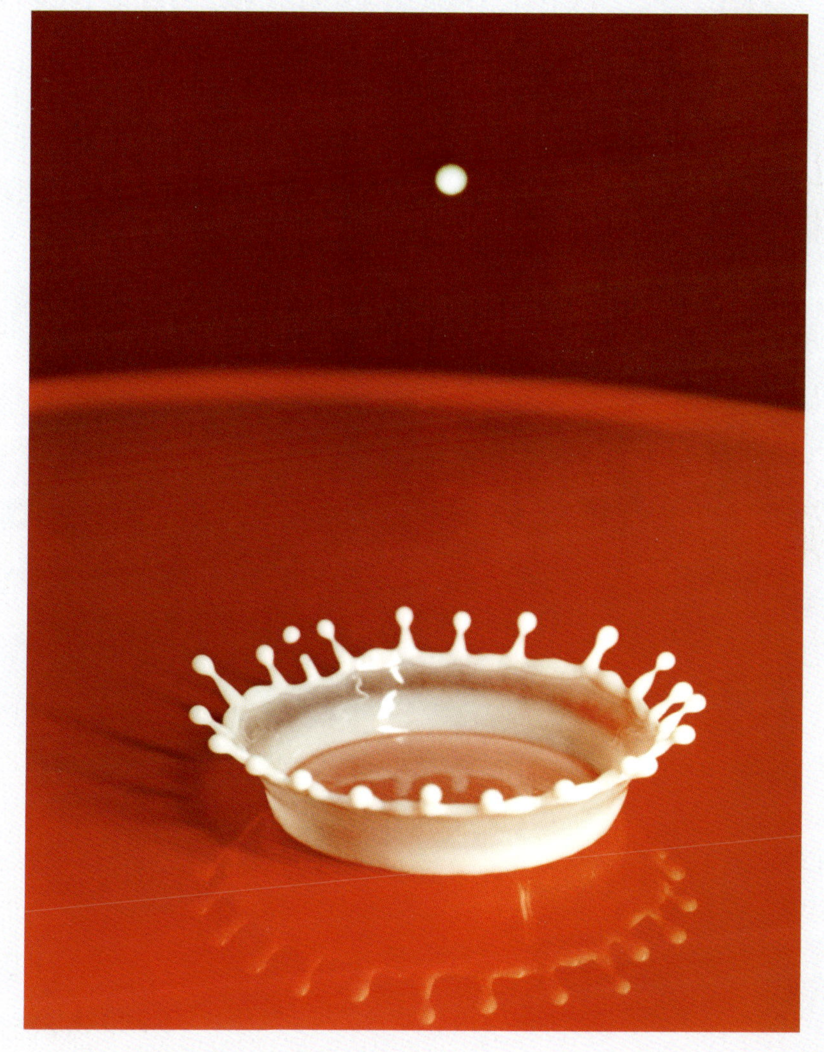

flashed on and off very much quicker than any shutter can open and close. A rapid flash of light is substituted for the opening and closing of a shutter and this burst of light not only provides the necessary range of speeds but also the intensity of illumination needed for photographic work. By repeating in a controlled way a rapid succession of flashes it is possible to record on one photograph and in **one multiple image the cumulative forms described by bodies moving through time. It is this effect, known as stroboscopic photography, for which Dr. Edgerton is best known. The stroboscope was invented in 1832. The discovery describes a phenomena whereby a moving object viewed either through a slotted disk or by flashes of light will appear, because of persistence of vision, either stationary, considerably slowed down**

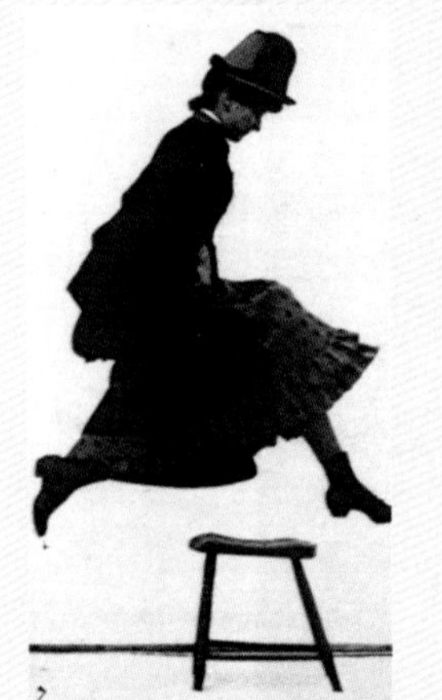

Pole Vaulter, David Tork. 1964. *Two multiflash strobes in trainable spot reflectors were directed on the vaulter Timing of the exposures was hand controlled. A camera with a fast-operating shutter was required to prevent blur from ambient light at Boston Garden*

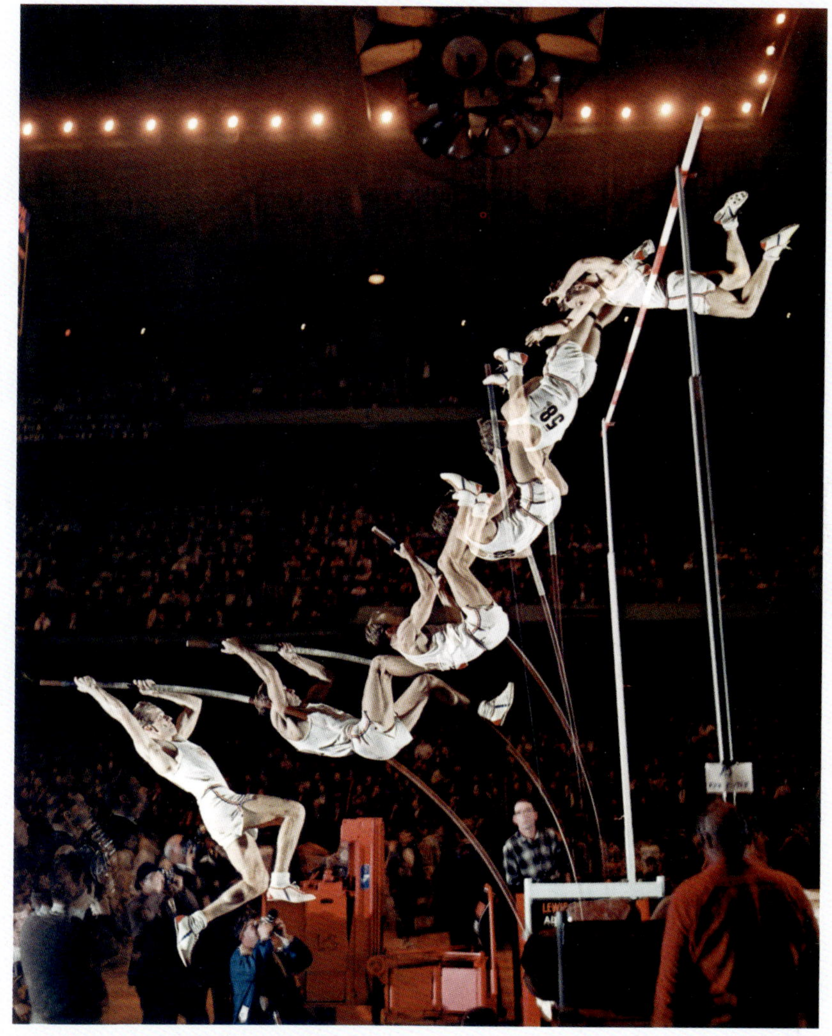

or even moving backwards. Dr. Edgerton's contribution in 1931 was to combine the camera and stroboscope. In addition he developed and perfected a stroboscope which could be controlled and timed accurately and which supplied in readily usable form the brilliant light necessary for this type of photographic work. Since the minute intervals between flashes may be

predetermined, stroboscopic photography presents for measurement and analysis phenomena that are too fast to be seen by the naked eye. One is able to record velocity, and acceleration of moving objects may be read and calculated from the photographs.

Dr. Edgerton, in either the single-flash or stroboscopic photographs, is working with exposures that range from a fifty thousandth of a second to a millionth of a

Swirls and Eddies of a Tennis Stroke. 1939

A multiflash study of a tennis stroke reveals the player as well as the racket and ball

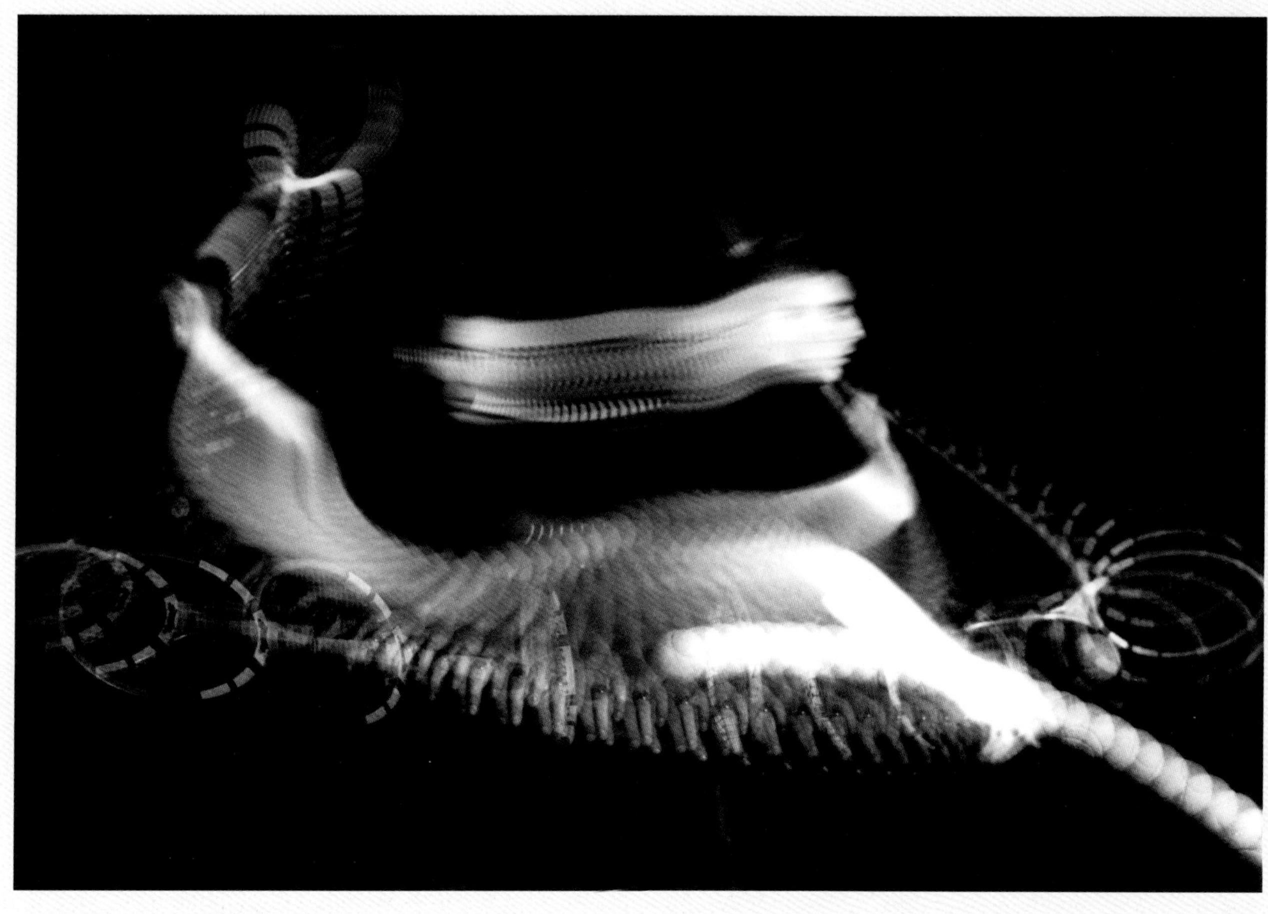

second. To produce a sharp photograph of a golf club striking the ball requires an exposure in the region of one hundred thousandth of a second. To investigate the dynamics of a bullet travelling at 1,800 miles per hour, an exposure of one millionth of a second is not too brief. Yet photographs taken at a 100,000th or even a millionth of a second whilst they may initially fire our curiosity, are not

intrinsically of any more value than those taken at more conventional speeds. Dr. Edgerton's work is remarkable because even at a millionth of a second his work has its own identity, quite as recognisable as those which distinguish more conventional photographers. His work has encompassed detailed and specialised research in electronics and yet his major photographic work has been the application of his high-

Golf Drive by Densmore Shute. 1938

A multiflash exposure of a white painted club against a black velvet background. The light frequency was 100 flashes per second

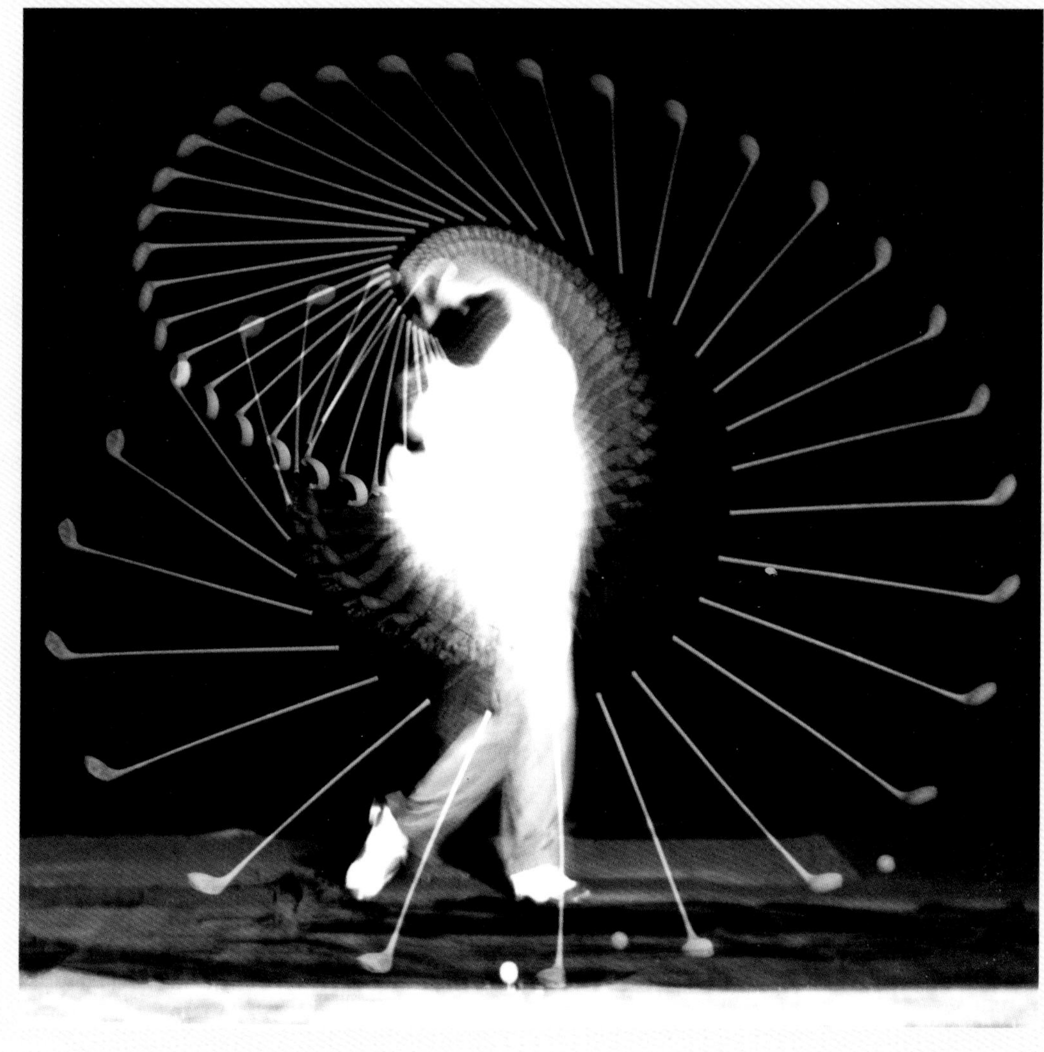

speed technique to everyday occurrences such as a tennis ball being struck, and a football being kicked, instances which in themselves are commonplace. Bullets, which are the very essence of high-speed are married to the mundane and pierce apples and blocks of soap or slice playing cards. That the bullet should slice a playing card, the texture, weight and feel of which is

known to all, rather than a blank sheet of graphed card is a measurable of Dr. Edgerton's skill in presenting a scientific demonstration in a memorable and comprehensible image. To the human eye these actions appear blurred or even invisible yet Dr. Edgerton through painstaking selection and clarity of his concerns presents us with photographs that are neatly conclusive as the lengthiest equations. These

Shock Waves from Impact. ca. 1965

This is a .30 caliber bullet shortly after it has broken a plexiglas target. The shock waves are made visible due to refraction of the light through the pressure region

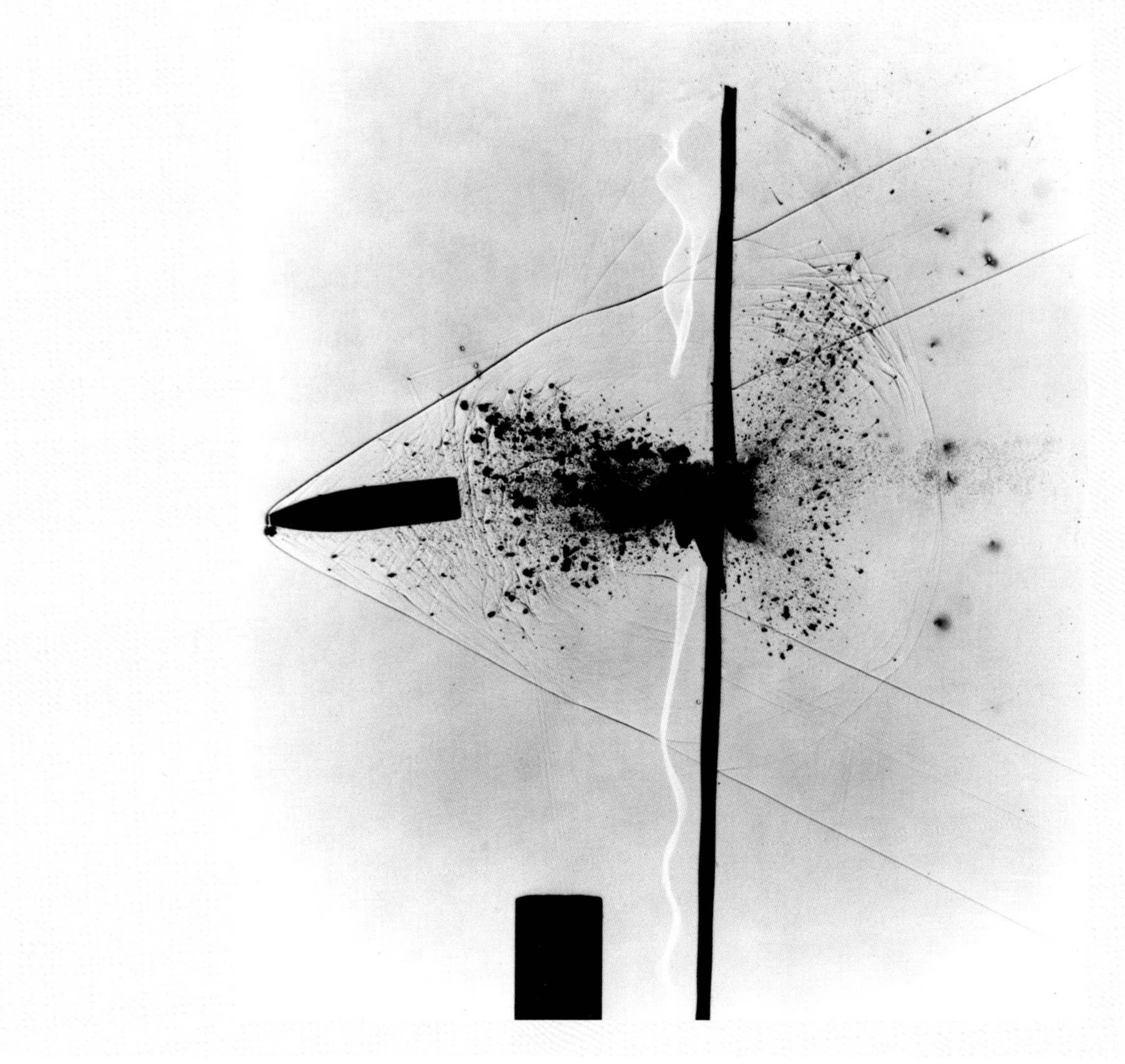

photographs endow us with new sight and they appeal because they allow us to see a kind of reality which we could never otherwise expect to see. The aesthetic aspects of science here appear in a universal language for all to appreciate. Yet the aesthetic is only one of the ways in which to discuss these photographs; Dr. Edgerton's comments and evaluations are often quite **different and more specific. It is in this respect that the titles and technical details of each photograph are so important. The structure of a bursting milk drop taken at a millionth of a second may well provide information of a kind different from the photograph of the same taken at half that speed. Dr. Edgerton is then first and foremost a scientist. Along with his colleagues, Germeshausen and Grier, he has for the last forty years been involved in research in**

Bullet and Apple. ca. 1964

A .30 caliber bullet is photographed shortly after it has penetrated an apple. The exposure time is about 0.5 microseconds

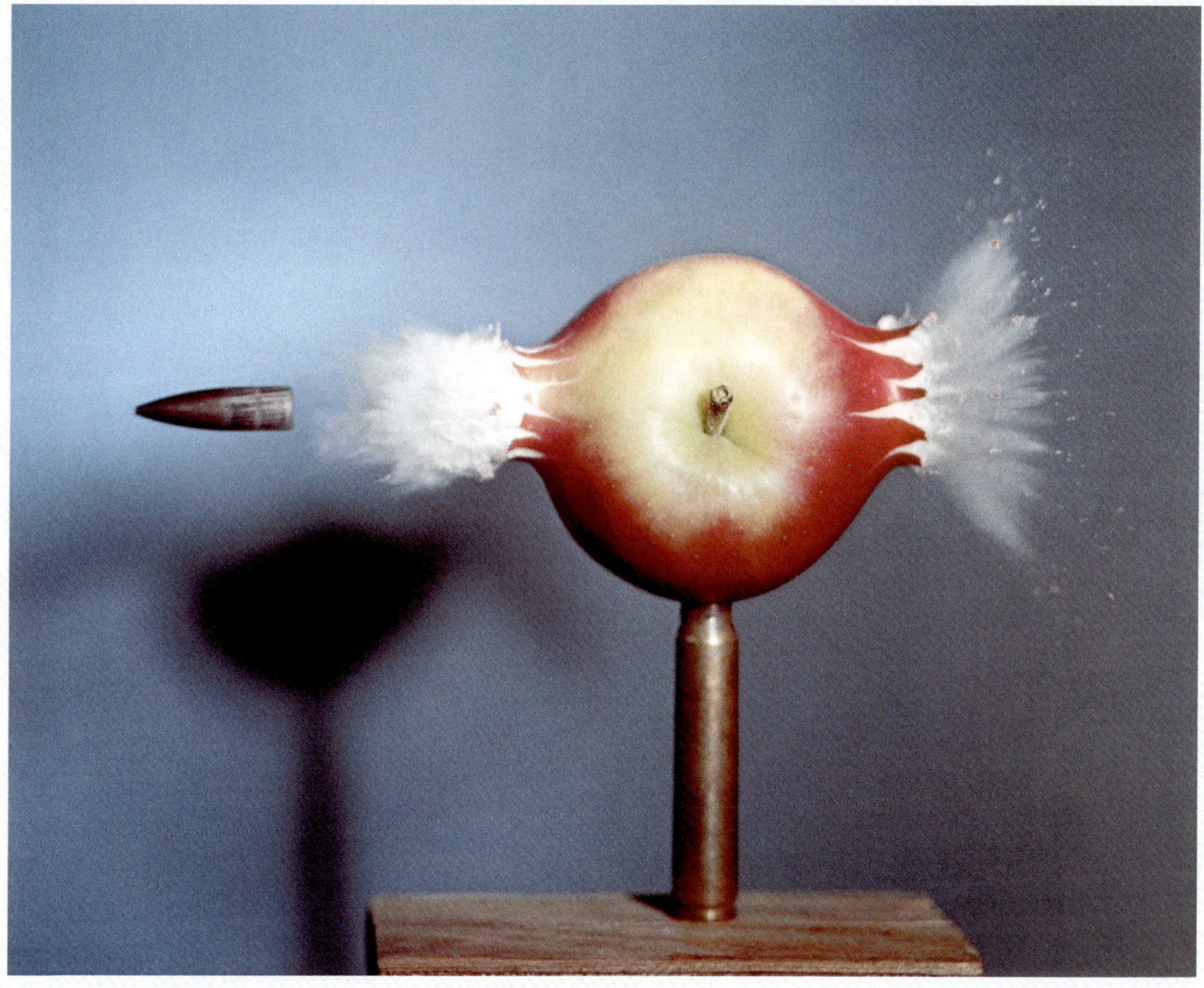

electrical engineering. These photographs are only the most accessible products of that lifetimes work.

Such is the power of these photographs that they have, within his own lifetime, become classic visual images. Almost everyone with an interest in the visual arts will know of the milk drop, golfer Shute or the bullet photographs and yet Dr. Edgerton's total work is almost unknown in this country. This neglect is unfortunate for Dr. Edgerton reminds us of the potential of the medium overlooked by an art dominated view of photography. Like the earliest pioneers of photography his work contains the element of magic and our response to these pictures must be similar to the disbelief, excitement and wonder that people must have felt when confronted with the first photographs.

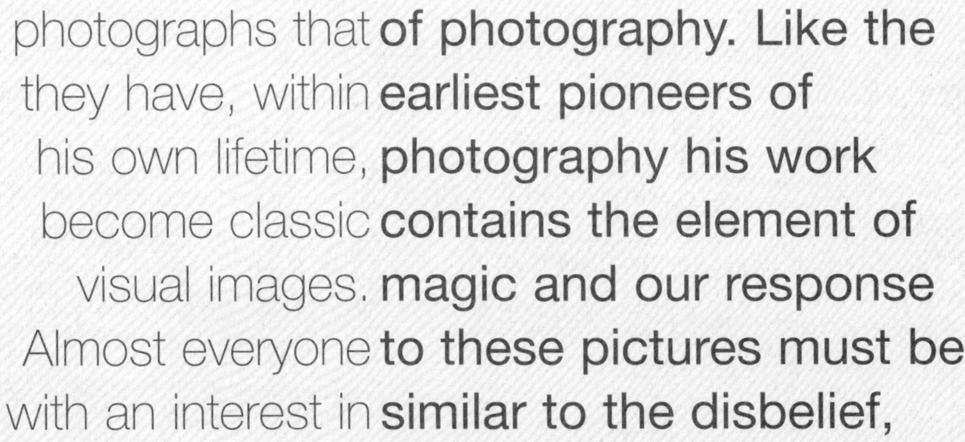

Geoffrey W. Holt *'Seeing the Unseen' exhibition catalogue, 1976*

Cutting the Playing Card Quickly. ca. 1964

The Jack of Diamonds is bisected by a .30 caliber bullet which has a speed of 2800 feet per second. The exposure time is about 0.5 microseconds (1/2,000,000 seconds)

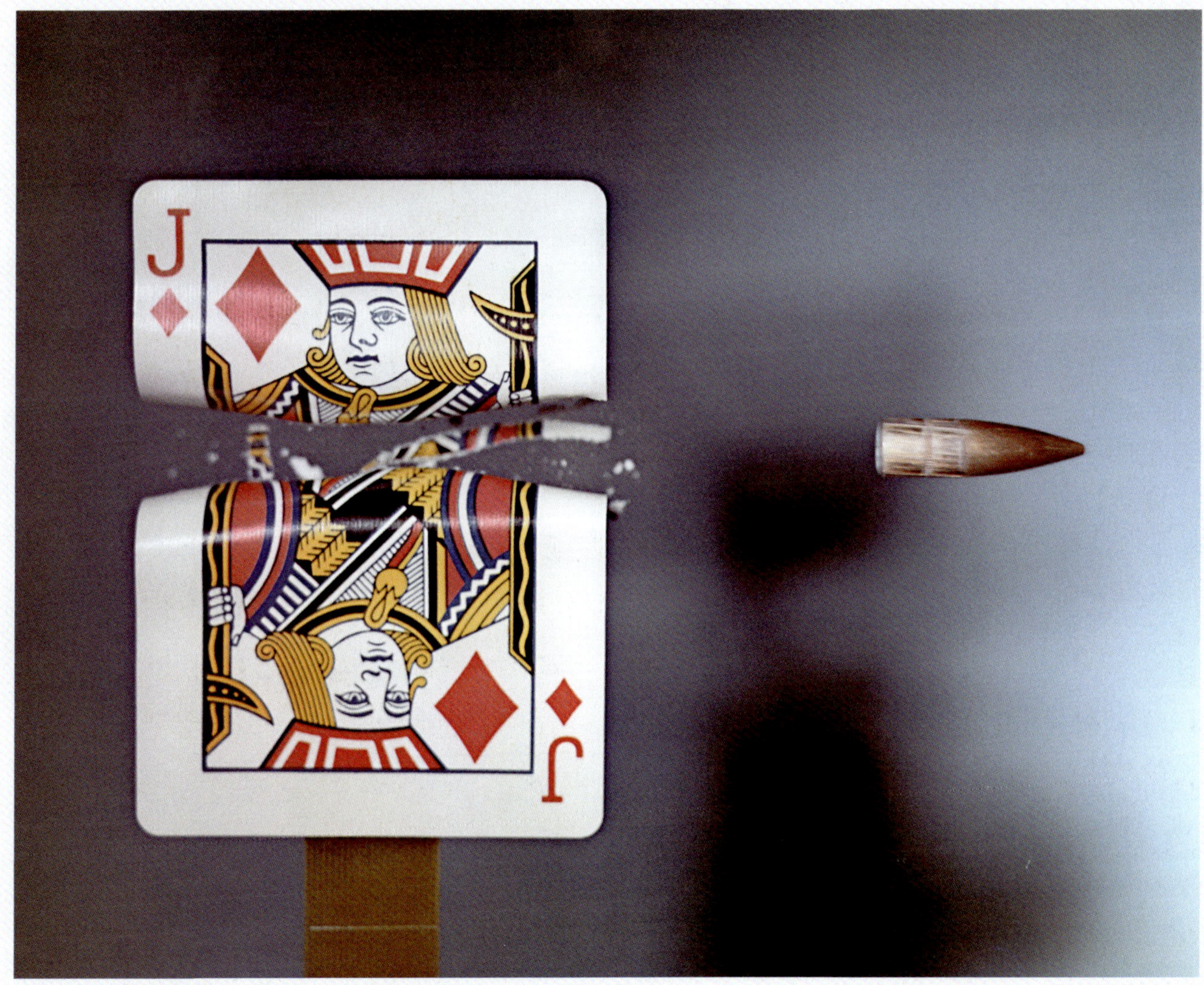
J
J

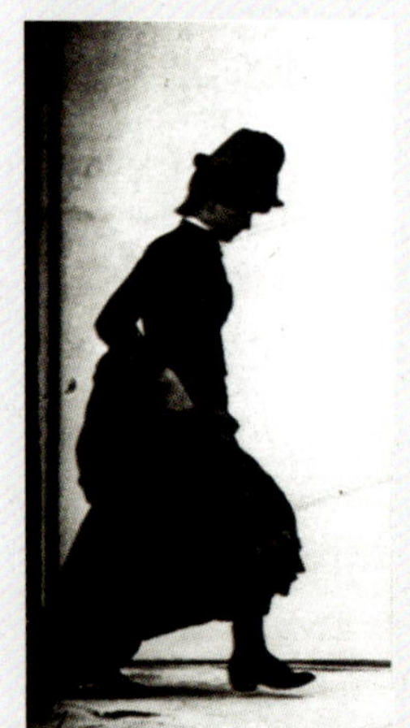

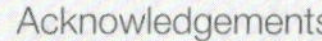

Acknowledgements

To all who participated during the residency and the main shoot. Reyahn King, Claire Harwood, James Cunliffe, Hannah Currin, Dale Orton, James Wiberley, Jonathan Stokes, Margaret & Christopher Shaw, the Shaw family, Catherine Tarbuck, Joe Holloway, John Spinks, Jon Dovey, Colin Alford's Processing Laboratories, William Wellesley-Davies, Will Barras, Tim Brayshaw, Mark Murphy, Peter Thompson, Karen Bird, Birmingham Royal Ballet, Birmingham Bullets, Coventry School of Art and Design, John Houchin @ Production Science, Manhattan Loft Corporation, Yacht Associates, Nigel Coates, Gerrard O'Carrol, Vivid, Artlounge, Dave Peebles @ Custard Factory, Why Not Associates, Andrew Willis, Pam Williams, Brian Gambles, Debra Klomp, formerly West Midlands Arts, Mark Dey, formerly West Midlands Arts, Mike Simkin, Geoffrey Holt, Martin Barnes V&A Museum, Gus Kyafas and Mary Steele, Palm Press, Harold & Esther Edgerton Foundation, Mark Wrenn & Mick Thacker, Tessa Sidey, David Rowan, Colin Edmonds and the technical team at BM&AG, Dave Lucas, Julia Kirby, Jan Anderson

First published in the UK in 2003 by
Dewi Lewis Publishing
8 Broomfield Road
Heaton Moor
Stockport SK4 4ND
+44 (0)161 442 9450
www.dewilewispublishing.com

in association with
Birmingham Library Services and Birmingham Museums & Art Gallery

ISBN: 1-904587-04-6

Design & artwork production: Jonathan Shaw
Printed by: EBS, Verona, Italy

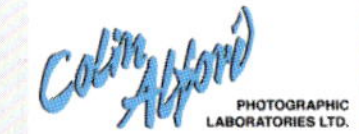

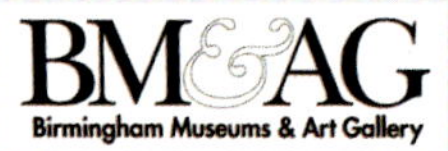

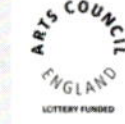

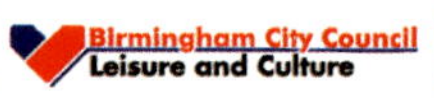

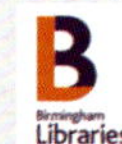

Plate 156. Movements. Jumping; running straight high jump; Model, 4 *(unmarried aged seventeen to twenty-four);* Costume, Draped. Fully clothed. 1887
Phases of Movement Illustrated. Laterals, 20 (12 illustrated for manual animation); Quantity of Movement, 1; Time, 103 Thousands of a Second